Developing You[ ]
Mathematical Learning Outdoors

Developing Young Children's Mathematical Learning Outdoors provides detailed guidance and practical advice on planning mathematical experiences for young children outdoors. By examining the key features of a mathematically rich outdoor environment, it illustrates how this can motivate children in leading their own learning and mathematical thinking.

Drawing upon the author's wealth of experience, the book provides support for students and early years' practitioners in developing a deeper understanding of how to plan quality experiences, which combine pedagogy with effective practice. Covering all aspects of mathematics, it identifies meaningful contexts and shows how adults can use open-ended questions and prompts to promote children's mathematical play outside.

With rich case studies and reflective questions included throughout, as well as suggestions for useful resources to put the ideas in the book into practice, it is essential reading for all those that want to develop curious and creative mathematical thinkers in the early years.

Lynda Keith is an education consultant, adviser and writer based in the UK. She has been involved in the teaching of early years' and primary maths at initial teacher education and in leading professional development for local authorities and individual school and nurseries for 40 years.

Developing Young Children's Mathematical Learning Outdoors

Linking Pedagogy and Practice

Lynda Keith

Routledge
Taylor & Francis Group

LONDON AND NEW YORK

First published 2018
by Routledge
2 Park Square, Milton Park, Abingdon, Oxon OX14 4RN

and by Routledge
711 Third Avenue, New York, NY 10017

Routledge is an imprint of the Taylor & Francis Group, an informa business

British Library Cataloguing-in-Publication Data
A catalogue record for this book is available from the British Library

Library of Congress Cataloging-in-Publication Data
Names: Keith, Lynda.
Title: Developing young children's mathematical learning outdoors : linking pedagogy
    and practice / Lynda Keith.
Description: Abingdon, Oxon ; New York, NY : Routledge, 2018. | Includes
    bibliographical references.
Identifiers: LCCN 2017006630 | ISBN 9781138237148 (hardback) | ISBN 9781138237155 (pbk.) |
    ISBN 9781315300672 (ebook)
Subjects: LCSH: Mathematics—Study and teaching (Elementary) | Mathematics—Study and
    teaching—Activity programs. | Outdoor education. | Early childhood education—Activity
    programs.
Classification: LCC QA135.6 .K45 2018 | DDC 372.7—dc23
LC record available at https://lccn.loc.gov/2017006630

ISBN: 978-1-138-23714-8 (hbk)
ISBN: 978-1-138-23715-5 (pbk)
ISBN: 978-1-315-30067-2 (ebk)

Typeset in Optima
by Apex CoVantage, LLC

Printed and bound by CPI Group (UK) Ltd, Croydon, CR0 4YY

Contents

Illustrations

Figure

Tables

Acknowledgements

I would like to thank the following early years' settings and people for their contributions to this book:

Auchnacraig Early Learning and Childcare Centre, West Dunbartonshire

Bright Horizons Nursery, Livingston

Corsehill Primary and Early Years Class, North Ayrshire

First Adventures Nursery, Linlithgow

Gavinburn Early Learning and Childcare Centre, West Dunbartonshire

Holy Cross Primary Nursery Class, North Lanarkshire

New Stevenson Primary Nursery Class, North Lanarkshire

Onthank Early Childhood Centre, East Ayrshire

St Luke's Primary Early Years Class, North Ayrshire

Woodlands Primary Nursery Class, Cumbernauld, North Lanarkshire

Ann MacFarlane, Early Years Team, North Ayrshire Council

I also greatly appreciate the feedback of impact on practice received on my courses and during visits to schools and early years' settings. This has helped to inform my own beliefs and confirm the value that I place on play as the most powerful way in which we can support early learning generally and in children's early mathematical development.

Finally, I would like to express my thanks to my husband, Derek, for all of his support during the writing of this book.

Introduction

The aim of this book is to provide those in teacher education and on early years training courses as well as existing practitioners with a deeper understanding of the mathematical knowledge and skills which underpin children's progression and development at such a vital stage in their life. Throughout the book, the term 'practitioner' will be used to include all staff and adults working with young children under 5 years old in a variety of settings. It also aims to explore what is meant by the pedagogy of early mathematical awareness and how young children make sense of what can be seen as a very abstract subject.

Using the outdoors as a rich environment for planning quality experiences, this book seeks to combine how young children learn best with the potential for meaningful mathematical learning opportunities. Links will be made across all aspects of maths, illustrating the connections that can arise through the careful balance of child-led and adult-initiated learning situations to support and enhance quality experiences. The role of the adult will be explored to enable you to consider the place of sustained shared thinking, using open-ended questioning, and prompts for thinking in promoting children's mathematical play.

It will identify meaningful contexts for learning which will help to motivate children in leading their own mathematical learning, thinking, talking and recording. Each chapter will include prompts for reflection and discussion points to enable you to consider the next steps for your own professional development. The key messages from these prompts will be collated in the last chapter as a final point of reflection.

A wide range of resources to support mathematical learning outdoors will be explored for their mathematical potential, and this will include everyday natural materials as well as specific resources, contexts for play, outdoor bags and boxes.

What types of young mathematical learners do we want?

I think that we need more bricks. Hundreds and hundreds to go up to the sky.
—Nursery child recreating the *Three Little Pigs'* house outdoors

There is an increasing focus on the potential for more outdoor play experiences for children at a time when many may have limited access and possibly more restricted learning indoors. With greater awareness of the importance of young children's health and well-being, the outdoor environment has had recent increased focus on its potential for children's overall development (Bilton, 2010). The Characteristics of Effective Learning in the Early Years Foundation Stage (EYFS) Statutory Framework in England (2012), *Building the Ambition: National Practice Guidance on Early Learning and Child-care, Children and Young People (Scotland) Act 2014* (Scottish Government, 2014), the revised Foundation Stage in Wales (2008) and Northern Ireland Curriculum (CCEA, 2006) clearly identify the importance of young children's learning on the need for play-based learning, exploration, building resilience, being active and engaged in the learning process, making decisions, making connections, thinking skills and creativity. All of these skills and dispositions are central to developing young children as mathematical thinkers and learners.

In addition, there has been wide-ranging exemplification within national guidance documentation and linked website pages to support practitioners in their practice. *Getting It Right for Play: The Power of Play – An Evidence Base* (2012) commissioned by Play Scotland discusses how children's play patterns in the outdoors have changed over time as many play spaces for children have become restricted. This document sets out the power of play in the outdoors for children's overall development. At a national level, Play Scotland is supporting play for all children and young people as part of the wider Scottish Government's Play Strategy. Similarly, the national charity Learning through Landscapes in England, Wales and Northern Ireland (Grounds for Learning) in Scotland supports schools and settings to enrich childhood by improving outdoor spaces. Its paper on core values for high quality outdoor experiences for young children identifies ten key features further explored in White et al. (2011). Each of these vision and value statements could also be clearly linked to the mathematical potential in the outdoors.

There also still remains a widespread culture of fear of maths at the adult level, and this has provided even more focus on the need to develop growth mindsets in young children. We know that they will learn best when they are happy, secure and can learn through play where there are no mistakes. How many of us may still have a fear of our own learning in maths – scared to try, unsure of what to do and quite a negative attitude which can remain with us for a long time? Boaler (2015) reminds us that we can't know what mathematics our children will need in the future but that the best preparation is to develop their mathematical ideas and help them to think in a flexible way, promoting problem solving and creativity.

The perception that it is OK to be 'no good at maths' and the many negative attitudes to maths in society are being increasingly challenged. The All Party Parliamentary Group for Maths and Numeracy (2016) identifies the difficulties for many parents to engage in mathematical experiences in the home due to embedded attitudes. The groups' paper on Maths and Numeracy in the Early Years concurs with the need to 'raise the profile of maths and encourage the development of mathematical thinking in young children.' It highlights the need to incorporate play into maths and the development of more concrete experiences for young children, especially in developing counting skills and a deeper understanding by practitioners in this key skill of number sense. In Scotland, one of the key areas for change comes from the Making Maths Count Group (2016) and focuses on transforming public attitudes to maths and in creating greater enthusiasm for maths as a vital life skill.

Based on our own experiences, it is also true that we can often focus on quite a narrow view of maths in our observations of children's play and can jump in too quickly with a question that we consider to be appropriate, e.g. 'How many is that?' when the child is not even considering the abstract nature of counting or whether it has a purpose in the nature of their play situation. We tend to see the maths curriculum as separate aspects, i.e. counting, shape, pattern, measure and information handling, but to the young child it is all learning. So in planning to meet their needs, we have to understand the links and connections in early mathematics, which will in turn help children to develop key skills and the confidence to apply their new-found knowledge and skills in different contexts. Central to developing our young learners is their motivation as mathematical thinkers, talkers and recorders – all of which will be necessary as the foundation of later learning in mathematics. Pound (2008) reminds us of the importance of these key aspects which will be further explored in Chapter 3. There is also a sense of maths being a boring subject and not in the least creative. On the contrary, Devlin (2000) argues that maths is full of creativity and about life. In thinking of maths only in terms of a worksheet or task to be completed, we risk gaining a full understanding of what children already know about the world and lose the possibilities to make 'the invisible visible' (Devlin, 2000) through quality interactions and appreciating this part of childhood as a time in its own right.

I spent a wonderful session with some 4-and-a-half-year-olds who had just started school, talking about what they knew about numbers, where they could find numbers and what numbers were for. Each child brought something different to these questions as they talked about their ages 'I'm 4 and will be bigger when I'm 5, but my brother is bigger still and he's 8'; numbers on buses 'I go on the number 45'; and 'I like big numbers. They've lots of zeros'. It brought me back to my firm belief that children have rich previous experiences upon which to build, but the most effective memories that children create are those that are truly embedded in their play with experiences in number, shape, measure and sorting and embedded in their own contexts to give real meaning. I am also more conscious of using the term 'experiences' rather than 'activities'. Influenced by Moyles (2013) and *Building the Ambition* (Scottish Government, 2014), experiences have a more qualitative feel for child-led learning, with deeper thinking involved than activity which may still be rich in learning but has the possibility of being highly planned with a very definite outcome in mind.

I have asked staff and students about the types of young mathematical learner we want to develop on many occasions, and their very varied responses are listed in Table 1.1.

In then asking about how young children learn best and develop a sound mathematical awareness, the following comments have been made, as shown in Table 1.2.

Table 1.1 What types of young mathematical learners do we want?

- Confident, engaged, focused
- Eager, motivated, enthusiastic
- Curious, investigative, inquisitive
- 'Have-a-go' attitude, resilient, tries different ways to solve a problem, risk taker
- Likes and seeks out challenges
- Open to suggestions
- Imaginative, creative
- Communicative, wants to talk about their learning
- Thinks things through, plans, predicts
- Sees real purposes for sorting, counting, measuring in contexts that make sense
- At times independent, but also cooperative and collaborative

Table 1.2 How do young children learn best and develop a sound mathematical awareness?

- By being actively engaged in their learning
- In rich play experiences
- Using open-ended resources which help them think differently
- Making choices and decisions about what they need
- With problems and challenges that are meaningful and playful to them
- Communicating in different ways – sometimes talking and reflecting; representing their ideas through mark making; sometimes revisiting their ideas
- By watching others and sharing ideas
- Getting a feel for numbers in their own way
- Starting with child-led ideas which are followed through by responsive adults

The outdoor environment should complement the mathematical learning occurring indoors, have equal value and offer mathematical opportunities which can't be:

- **achieved indoors,** e.g. due to restriction in size and scope of materials. This would include the use of construction with large crates and pallets, experiences that will take up an extended space, water and sand investigations which extend beyond one indoor water tray to enable exploration of longer tubing and linking builders' trays or connecting to a hose pipe. Learning mathematically outdoors will also enhance the experiences of real seasonal change and the understanding of time, which can be more limited in scope through pictures indoors. If early mathematical awareness requires children to make links, where can it be done more effectively than in this context?

- **achieved in the same way,** e.g. selection of loose parts for creative investigations, sorting with different resources in different ways, measuring for different purposes, locating objects and developing spatial awareness through physical play in a different environment with different levels to explore and to enhance different perspectives, and recording opportunities in mark making.

- **achieved to offer new and challenging opportunities** with natural resources, real habitats and real-life contexts for visits and shopping. New opportunities will therefore lead to new ways of thinking mathematically, applying the skills from indoor learning, and vice versa, and adapting resources to be used in a new way in different play situations, e.g. den building. It is an environment in which children can be noisier and messier, and it offers a freedom to be more innovative and creative in and with the environment.

Outdoor learning in maths will also complement an investigative approach to learning mathematically which starts with experiences that can be offered, rather than simply different resources and equipment. The child is at the centre of the interaction with the environment, and it is necessary to observe carefully how different children will adapt, apply and learn differently in an outdoor context.

There are very sound links between young children's schematic patterns of behaviour in what they play with and how they play with it repeatedly and early mathematical development Hughes (2010). We, therefore, need to consider how the experiences we offer outside can support and enhance the quality of experiences we offer indoors for this type of learning to continue.

Table 1.3 Schema in the outdoors

Schema	What could be the potential for early mathematical development outdoors?
Transporting	As they move objects from one place to another, children will be involved in making decisions about where they go, how to fill containers, how to move, and what to carry, and they will develop skills in reasoning about whether something is too heavy or too big, thereby involving themselves in risk assessment through their mathematical play.
Positioning	As they line up objects and look for similar or different sized objects, children are using skills in ordering and are developing language skills in positional language.
Enclosing	In using large block play and creating their own play spaces with tyre surrounds, children are developing their skills in spatial awareness, in creating borders which, in turn, will lead to an understanding of perimeter at a later stage of their development. The real and very active involvement of physical play outdoors cannot be underestimated as a valid and valuable concrete learning experience prior to children's developmental stages in pictorial representation and in leading to more abstract concepts.
Assembling	As children develop their large construction play outdoors, the variation in materials to stack, pile up and line up engages them in the problem solving process where visualisation becomes more prevalent in enabling children to think something through.
Enveloping	The dens that children create outdoors, that is, their choice of covering, measuring to fit and hiding under covers, are a prerequisite to children's early understanding of area and appropriateness of shape and space.
Connecting and separating	As children build on their curiosity to investigate what fits/doesn't fit, what they need to connect and what happens when they take something apart to try a different way or material, they develop the thinking processes that play a large part in early problem solving development. Children also begin to ask questions more readily, perhaps not orally but certainly in the decision making process happening in their minds as they select and refine their ideas.
Horizontal, vertical and diagonal movement	The mathematical potential of position and movement is developed further in the outdoors as children explore lines, make markings, climb up and down, throw balls in different directions, and play with ribbons to begin thinking about patterns in a real context.
Rotating	Quality experiences in exploring how to turn objects, which objects turn or roll either in the use of tyres or water wheels, using hoops and creating circles in a game all help to build on earlier understanding of properties of objects and a more creative and different way of thinking about sorting in their own way and for their own purposes.

Photo 1.1 Exploring what fits in the baking tray

Photo 1.2 Investigating the patterns within the wheels

Photo 1.3 What goes round and round? Finding similar properties

As we explore the types of mathematical learners we want, how they develop mathematically in the most effective ways and the importance of the continuity of an approach that is embedded in play and play-based learning, how do we justify and define pedagogy when there can be the pressure of targets or outcomes which, although important, may lead to rushing into a more formalised approach that is not suited to meeting the needs of children? *Building the Ambition* (Scottish Government, 2014) defines pedagogy as 'the interactions and experiences which support the curriculum and the process of how children learn'. As Curriculum for Excellence in Scotland is designed for children from 3 to 18, it is necessary that these early mathematical experiences lay a strong foundation for later development and that they are 'integrated, in meaningful contexts and developmentally appropriate'. This is endorsed by the curriculum in New Zealand. *Early Mathematics: A Guide for Improving Teaching and Learning,* published by the Education Review Office (2016), focuses on the need for strong subject knowledge about mathematics in early childhood in order to be innovative in planning learning for young children. Research in Ireland (Dooley et al., 2014) describes the 'powerful nature of play and mathematics as fundamental to good mathematical pedagogy in early childhood'.

In *Let's Talk About Pedagogy: Towards a Shared Understanding for Early Years Education in Scotland* (Scottish Executive, 2005), the authors reiterate the point about making the why of our practice visible – our need to justify what we do we and how we do it, explain to parents and carers, the need to be evidence-based in our own understanding and to draw upon the influences of our practice from research and background reading. All of this helps to inform our practice so that we can have a shared understanding as to our role in children's mathematical development. One of the recommendations for the Early Years Foundation Stage in England from the Tickell report (2011) was to place a focus on how children learn, rather than what they learn. This led, in the revised EYFS (2012), to the Characteristics of Effective Learning, defined as:

By playing and exploring (engagement)

    Finding out and exploring

    Using what they know in their play

    Being willing to have a go

Active learning (motivation)

    Being involved and concentrating

    Keeping on trying

    Enjoying achieving what they set out to do

Creating and thinking critically (thinking)

    Having their own ideas

    Making links

    Choosing ways to do things

These learning characteristics are about processes rather than outcomes; therefore, the processes underpinning the rich understanding in early maths require the same quality of focus in our observations as any intended goals or outcomes. The intrinsic motivation, curiosity and skill in finding their own ways to make sense of maths must be central to developing this pedagogy into practice. Moylett (2013) also discusses further how many of the characteristics are indeed skills and learning strategies for life.

The curriculum in Northern Ireland places emphasis on promoting thinking skills and personal capabilities across the curriculum in the foundation stage, and these are also fundamental to early mathematical development. The core skills include:

- Thinking, problem solving and decision making
- Managing information
- Being creative
- Working with others
- Self-management

The curriculum is also embedded in a play-based learning philosophy, well evidenced through the work of researchers at Stranmillis University College, Belfast. The Thinking Skills in the Early Years report commissioned by the CCEA (Walsh et al., 2007) sets out very clearly these underpinning skills necessary for all mathematical learners and in creating the quality of environments necessary for these to be developed indoors and outside. In Chapter 2 we will look in more detail at the environment needed to create contexts for learning outdoors, and in Chapter 3 we explore in more detail the developmental stages in early mathematical awareness to examine how outdoor learning can provide the anticipated outcomes in learning that we want to achieve, in that they match children's learning best and have a focus on the balance of mathematical and child development at the heart of quality experiences.

In summary, if we consider the pedagogy of early mathematical awareness in terms of how the learning and teaching can be facilitated, then we need to consider how to plan for quality experiences which are mathematically meaningful, through our interactions, in evaluating the outdoor environment and in the knowledge that young children will learn in very different ways and at different rates.

Points for reflection and discussion

1   What are your own experiences of and feelings about maths? How might these influence your work with young children?

2   What recurring themes of how young children learn best in maths arise in this chapter?

3   How can we start to think about how to support young children as mathematical learners?

References

All Party Parliamentary Group for Maths and Numeracy (2016) *Maths and Numeracy in the Early Years*. Available at: www.appgmathsnumeracy.org.uk

Bilton, H. (2010) *Outdoor Learning in the Early Years Management and Innovation* (3rd edition). London. David Fulton Publishers.

Boaler, J. (2015) *The Elephant in the Classroom: Helping Children Learn and Love Maths*. London. Souvenir Press.

CCEA (2006) *Understanding the Foundations Phase*. Belfast. CCEA.

Cole-Hamilton, I. (2012) *Getting It Right for Play: The Power of Play – An Evidence Base*. Midlothian. Play Scotland.

Department for Education (2012) *Statutory Framework for the Early Years Foundation Stage: Setting the Standards for Learning, Development and Care for Children from Birth to Five*. Available at: http://www.foundationyears.org.uk/eyfs-statutory-framework/

Devlin, K. (2000) *The Maths Gene: Why Everyone Has it but Most People Don't Use it*. London. Phoenix.

Dooley, T., Dunphy, E. and Shiel, G. (2014) *Dublin Research Report No. 18: Mathematics in Early Childhood and Primary Education (3–8 years) Teaching and Learning*. National Council for Curriculum and Assessment.

Early Education (2012) *Development Matters in the Early Years Foundation Stage*. London. Early Education.

Education Review Office (2016) *Early Mathematics: A Guide for Improving Teaching and Learning*. New Zealand Government. New Zealand.

Hughes, A. (2010) *Developing Play for the Under 3s*. London. David Fulton Publishers.

Moyles, J. (2013) 'Empowering Children and Adults: Play and Child-Initiated Learning' in Featherstone, J. (ed.), *Supporting Child-Initiated Learning: Like Bees Not Butterflies*. London. Featherstone.

Moylett, H., ed. (2013) *Characteristics of Effective Learning: Helping Young Children Become Learners for Life*. London. Open University Press.

Pound, L. (2008) *Thinking and Learning about Mathematics in the Early Years*. London. Routledge.

Scottish Executive (2005) *Let's Talk about Pedagogy: Towards a Shared Understanding for Early Years Education in Scotland*. Dundee. Learning and Teaching Scotland.

Scottish Government (2014) *Building the Ambition: National Practice Guidance on Early Learning and Childcare, Children and Young People (Scotland) Act 2014*. Edinburgh. APS Group Scotland.

Scottish Government (2016) *Transforming Scotland into a Maths Positive Nation: Final report of the Making Maths Count Group*. Edinburgh. Making Maths Count Group.

Tickell, C. (2011) *The Early Years: Foundations for Life, Health and Learning: An Independent Report on the Early Years Foundation Stage to Her Majesty's Government*. London. Department of Education.

Walsh, G., Murphy, P., Dunbar, C. in collaboration with EYEcep team. (2007) *Thinking Skills in the Early Years: A Guide for Practitioners*. Belfast. Stranmillis University College.

Welsh Assembly Government (2008) *Foundation Phase Framework for Children's Learning for 3–7-year-olds in Wales*. Wales. Welsh Government.

White, J. (Ed.) (2011) *Outdoor Provision in the Early Years*. London. Sage Publications.

2 | What are the key features of a mathematically enriched outdoor environment?

I've got £500 in my purse. I need to get some money on my card so that I can buy loads of things. Can I take my dog? He is well trained. How much will it be? It will be £5. My money has gone up to £800. I'm going to Florida as well as Legoland.
—Nursery child aged 4, talking about shopping outdoors.

When we develop an outdoor environment in an early years' setting, do we look at it in the same way as we perhaps may analyse the areas within the playroom? In taking a closer look at the outdoors and the potential for enhancing and extending mathematical learning, what else does it offer to young children? As a natural place for learning with different resources and the space to play in different ways and investigate and combine materials, the outdoors offers richness in opportunities for sorting, matching, collecting information, problem solving, finding patterns and shapes, and using positional language within a different setting. This, in turn, leads to young children asking more questions, often thinking deeper as they practise skills in trial and error, in cause and effect and in developing creative solutions to problems they encounter through their play.

The chapter is illustrated with photos of different parts of the outdoor environment, alongside discussion of the mathematical potential of each, e.g. bike tracks, planting and growing, water investigations, sand investigations, large block play and construction, the mud kitchen and den building.

What do we need to consider in developing a mathematically rich outdoor learning environment?

Based on the discussion in Chapter 1, we need to take into consideration:

- the type of mathematical learner we want
- what we know about how young children learn best mathematically

- the physical layout of the space that we have available in the immediate outdoors and beyond.

All outdoor areas and spaces are entirely different, and normally we have to work with the area and space we have. Whilst it is desirable that there is free flow between the indoor and outdoor environments, this is not always achievable due to staffing, location and the numbers of children within the establishment. We do have to be careful, however, not to lose in any way the children's motivation and must encourage their ideas to be recorded through idea and suggestion boards and as part of the planning process.

Due to the recent focus generally on outdoor learning, there has been more support in documentation and background website reading to support the organisation of space and creating playful spaces for children. In the UK alone, publications have been produced at the national and local levels as schools and early years' settings consider the potential of the outdoors.

> Developing mathematical thinking and learning mathematical skills can and should be part of children's everyday experiences. They can count, measure and explore shapes, and develop their understanding of mathematical concepts and numerical reasoning in context. In fact, all the mathematical learning children do indoors they can also do outdoors, but with vigour, freedom and scale.
>
> *Further Steps Outdoors: Guidance* (Welsh Government, 2014)

Building the Ambition (Scottish Government, 2014) promotes an environment that will promote curiosity, inquiry and creativity. In the descriptor for what an environment for young children needs, it includes 'invites discussion with interesting objects to talk about and explore, stimulating curiosity', and it also identifies the importance of giving the young child time to 'persevere with their thinking and inquiries, to test their own theories out over several days or re-examine the same experiences again over time in a variety of ways (Scottish Government, 2014).

Mathematical concepts are not developed quickly. In Chapter 3 we will see how these are developmental, have layers of learning from the very early concrete experiences to more abstract thought and cannot be rushed without gaps beginning to appear, especially in the depth of children's experiences. This new and different world of the outdoors offers new and linked experiences for which we need to ensure equity of access for all children.

Planning for children outdoors is about focusing on the possible learning opportunities, not just the 'activity' or setting up places that might have the potential for learning without ensuring that learning occurs. The children need to be involved in the setting up of outdoor areas. They are more than capable of sharing their ideas, making choices and decisions and being actively involved in the setting up of the area, from planning to physically helping to create areas. The word 'experience' denotes the fact that children may bring something to their learning based on prior knowledge and that it is about the engagement level within that experience which makes the difference in the outcome. Often the outcome with early mathematics can be even richer than one that is highly focused and can lead to more of an anticipated outcome or possible lines of development.

Mathematical conversations occur naturally among children during play outdoors. We need to tune in to the children's play and see the opportunities for mathematical learning as we go along, and perhaps create an area that meets both the children's and our philosophy of how they learn best. If we are lucky, and truly observe and listen to children, we can be active participants in their play and observe authentic and experiential learning whilst still meeting the experiences and outcomes outlined in national guidance for maths in the early years.

It may help to think of our outside area in much the same way we think of our indoor setting. We arrange our indoor settings into areas – book/reading corner, role play area, maths area, creative area, etc. – areas which have been organised and planned for a specific purpose or activity. We also give due consideration to the natural flow for play experiences when arranging the space where possible, e.g. construction area near to the maths area.

It may be helpful to think about how we organise our outside environment into learning areas that provide a specific learning focus but at the same time allow for flexibility and movement between spaces and in the wide ranging use of resources within them. By doing this, we can offer access to the whole curriculum through a balance of experiences which take maths across all areas of learning where appropriate. Children should not see maths as a separate subject. It is an aspect of learning with strong transferrable skills, particularly in problem solving as a life skill. The place of problem solving will permeate the book but is discussed more fully in Chapter 3.

In considering how best to provide for all aspects of mathematical learning and how to create links and connections for children in a more holistic way, we may consider an overview plan which may comprise:

- a planting and growing area
- a wheeled toys area for bikes and tracks
- a water/sand area
- a large construction and block play area
- a mud kitchen area

- a den building area; and
- a climbing and physical play area.

What can be achieved will also be influenced by any large and permanent structures in place within the outdoor area. At the end of the chapter, some of these potential areas will be explored for their mathematical potential. The commitment to involving children in the decision making about what could be in the outdoor area is in itself a huge learning opportunity. On one of my many visits to early years' centres, I was engaged in a discussion with the children about their decision to have a stage outside. They wanted to sing their rhymes and be able to do so more vocally than they could inside! Needless to say, this play was extended to create a plan for what the stage could look like. A list of resources was generated, with children realising that they had to sort out what was possible and what was not. For example, they wanted real curtains on a pulley like in a theatre, and this had to be improvised using what we had! The nature of this symbolic play shows creativity in itself as children try to work out alternatives.

Therefore, we need to let children be involved in evaluation and planning. Is there a day for a special learning event? If we want to throw balls, where is the safest place to do it? Why? How can we all get to the loose parts centre without disrupting someone else's play? What's the best place for the bikes and wheeled toys? Do we need stopping spaces for safety? These are all real-life questions which are the basis of real maths in the child's world.

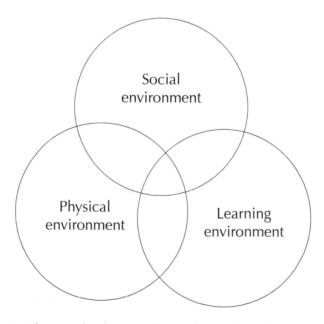

Figure 2.1 The interrelated nature of an outdoor mathematical environment

The social environment

In a mathematical, social environment (Figure 2.1), each child's contributions are valued and respected. This is critical for later development in collaborative approaches. It is a safe place to try things out, but with agreed rules for safety, caring for each other and looking after each other. The social environment is about developing the positive attitudes and growth mindsets required for maths, i.e. children will be supported when things don't work out but will be encouraged to try again or in a different way.

Children should also have ownership of the resources and encouraged to take responsibility for their storage and organisation. Their ideas can be actively sought about what should be in the outdoor area and in drawing up the rules for everyone. At St Luke's Primary Nursery Class, the children created a set of rules for themselves and for teachers and other adults. For each other, these included:

- You need to see the teachers, and they need to see you.
- We still need to stay quite close. Don't go out the gates, EVER!
- Any broken bit, if we can't fix it, has to go in the bin.
- We need our listening ears.

Draw up rules for the class together.

For the teachers and other adults the rules included:

- The teachers listen. They like to hear laughing. They don't like to hear us crying.
- Keep your eyes switched on.
- Any broken bits, the teachers have to take them away.
- Teachers need to count the children lots of times.
- Stop at the gates, and only the teachers open and close the gates.

More of the case study about their journey of change will be found in Chapter 6.

In the social environment, a very positive attitude is promoted towards early mathematical awareness, the underpinning skills and dispositions of resilience, and creativity and curiosity. It is a socially constructed environment, with adults who value how children best make sense of mathematics and numeracy, balancing the child's world and real-life situations. It is important that the children see adults counting and mark making for a variety of purposes and using numbers in different situations outdoors. This is an environment for new questions with different kinds of language, so are the questions and prompts for thinking that we use sufficiently differentiated to meet the needs of all children? When children begin to use new language through their outdoor mathematical play, how do we help them make links with indoor experiences? This will be further explored in Chapter 4.

In 'Assessing the Quality of Early Learning Environments' (Walsh and Gardner, 2005), nine key themes, such as motivation and independence, are identified as representing significant aspects of a high-quality environment for learning. The others are summarised by the following keywords:

- motivation
- concentration
- independence
- confidence
- well-being
- social interaction
- respect
- multiple skill acquisition
- higher-order thinking skills.

We will consider throughout the book how these may be evident in our outdoor planning for early mathematical awareness.

The physical environment

The physical environment for mathematical development should be a welcoming place for children to play, with experiences that totally embed their thinking across all of the outdoors, not just in one area. Some children need quiet places for reflection to think of an idea, so it is often useful to consider a thinking zone within a sometimes very busy and physically active environment. How has the layout been decided? How do we create boundaries? How do children decide and get involved in creating signs for outdoors? Do the resources include plenty of natural materials for children to explore and be creative in handling and exploring materials with which they may be unfamiliar in any other context? Is there always free access to mark making materials to encourage and support their own ideas in their play? The value of mark making will be explored further in Chapter 4.

The learning and teaching environment

Here are some key questions to consider in taking forward a quality outdoor environment for early maths:

- What makes it an interesting, engaging, organised yet flexible environment where children have discussed how to use the resources and investigated their potential?

- Where are there opportunities for children to develop curiosity, creativity and inquiry?
- How do we translate the mathematical 'curriculum' into quality experiences for children to take their learning forward?
- Are there plenty of loose-part materials for children to use in their play to enable deeper thinking and create more choices?
- Are all staff motivated to want to explore the outdoors and understand the relevance of outdoor mathematical learning? Or are the views of maths restricted to simply the recognition of shapes and numbers without giving due consideration to the pedagogy appropriate to this age group, developmentally appropriate practice and, most importantly, hooking children into maths?
- If children learn best by observing, talking, communicating and sharing their ideas in different ways, how do we promote this within the environment?
- Do they have opportunities to investigate, revisit, repeat, practise and extend?
- How do we enable children to reflect on their learning and celebrate achievement?
- Is the environment a place where questions are asked, explored, answered, shared and enjoyed?

These questions will form part of a final audit in Chapter 7.

In considering the key features of turning pedagogy into practice in terms of the social, physical, and teaching and learning environment, here are 12 indicators to reflect on what is important in young children's mathematical development:

1 Provides flexible areas.

Although there may be specific areas in which resources are located at the start of a session, it is important that there is a shared understanding about children's need to transport objects for their own reasons to enhance their play. This may not always be physically possible, and children should know when to ask to take things, whether it is safe to do so and to take them back at the end of the play. Flexibility does allow for more freedom and creativity particularly when children are able to justify their choice of resource for a planned reason.

2 Enables children to link different aspects of mathematical play.

Mathematical play enables children to develop a greater awareness of the properties and features of resources, what they can do with them, what is useful and what is not. As they explore shape, they can make links to pattern. As they count, they develop a greater mastery of what quantity means. As they play, they can work out how to record information in a way that is meaningful to the play context.

3   Develops choice and decision making.

In early maths, children may need to decide what is the best tool to dig in the sand, to mix in the mud kitchen or to gather materials from the loose parts area for their construction. As a skill, this deepens children's thinking and evaluative skills about why it may have been the best resource or step, consider other alternatives and think about a quicker or easier solution. This is key to later development when children will be required to choose which strategy they will use to perform a calculation or solve a problem. The stage of trial and error in a safe environment encourages children to take a risk, refine their ideas and justify their solution. This process development is an essential skill which demands more that just reaching a solution.

4   Offers challenge and problem solving opportunities.

Pound (2008) notes that the importance of problem solving should not be underestimated but that children are also problem finders and that this curiosity is what adults wanting to support children in their mathematical development should be seeking to foster. In our interactions with children, we need to put a positive focus on problem solving as part of everyday life.

5   Enables children to make sense of the mathematical world around them.

By exploring in a way that brings children into contact with different natural materials and seasonal changes, they look more closely at their surroundings and what they have to offer.

6   Starts from the child's curiosity and freedom to investigate.

Curiosity is still the start point in early maths to children's intrinsic motivation to want to find out, count, measure, compare and sort for their own purposes.

7   Promotes new language in new contexts and language of inquiry.

From the curiosity comes the questions, usually why? or what? types of questions. We also want to promote questions of prediction and evaluation so that children can take their own levels of inquiry to a deeper level and challenge themselves.

8   Offers opportunities to develop mathematical skills across the areas.

Consider using the continuous provision chart in Chapter 6 to start thinking about the maths that could be developed in each area and this, in itself, will start to show the depth of how skills, knowledge and understanding can be applied across the areas. Sorting with the water play materials will have very different purposes and language and challenge opportunities in different areas of continuous provision.

9 **Provides open-ended resources to support all aspects of mathematical learning.**

The more open the resource, the more open the scope for mathematical thinking and creativity. It helps for us to try to see the world as the child does and also to mix up different resources within to observe how they interact with them.

10 **Offers a fun active and challenging environment which promotes active thinking.**

What makes the learning more challenging? It is not necessarily something more difficult or more formalised or focused on moving onto the next stage of development. Challenge has to be something that we want children to enjoy, not fear or link negative connotations with the word.

11 **Encourages multisensory learning.**

The outdoor mathematical environment should provide opportunities for children to touch, feel, smell, climb, examine, hear and bring all of the senses to the experiences. Children are sorting as they select from a choice of spoons or choose which pot or pan to strike to make their music. The sensory garden provides experiences in sorting that can't be replicated to the same extent indoors and to explore and dig in the earth provides a greater scale of understanding about measure and area.

12 **Values children's mathematical graphics and recording.**

Surfaces that can allow children to mark make with chalk, large pens or squirty water bottles can be the greatest canvas upon which to create. If mark making is seen to have purpose and sufficiently varied resources are available, then children will want to record in their own ways to make marks which are meaningful to the play situation. This early stage of creating will lead to an understanding of mathematical symbols that have a more abstract meaning.

Taking a closer look at possible areas and their potential for mathematical development

Creating a focused area for maths

Although the play opportunities for maths will be available across the entire outdoor environment, there is also scope for a maths based area which may complement the area indoors. The resources within this area would still offer flexibility, choice and an open-ended approach. The photographs below show how one setting created an area for exploration and discovery.

Photo 2.1 Developing a maths area outdoors

Photo 2.2 Resources for investigation in the area

Photo 2.3 Making choices and decisions

Photo 2.4 Designing an obstacle course

Bikes, tracks and transporting

Table 2.1 Bikes, tracks and transporting

Possible resources	Potential for mathematical learning
Bikes Scooters	Developing the language of direction: moving forwards, backwards, turn left, right, stop, start, round, reverse, start, finish
Wheelbarrows Clothes horse	Changing speed – fast, slow, going faster, slower. Making decisions about when and why you need to slow down, when it is safer to go a little faster
Tubs or hooks for helmets	Estimating: which bike will go fastest? Will it be the one with big wheels or small wheels? How far to the finishing line?
Signs Cones	Investigating the pattern made with tyre tracks, through the water, through puddles. Talking about where the pattern will go and how far will it reach before the water runs out or disappears.
Timers	Sorting to find out whether there is a helmet for each child on the bike/scooter. Children mark making on the tubs and creating signs to remind everyone that they need a helmet for safety.
	Children using numbers, letters, symbols to make registration plates and developing a system for parking bikes, e.g. number 1 bay for number 1 bike.
	Creating a petrol station: developing a sense of money and exchange.
	Using a timer to ensure a fair share of time on the bikes and developing a sense of time. Posing the question "how long until your turn?" and using mathematical language of next, after, soon.

Photo 2.5 How can you create an environment to combine different resources on the tracks and build on children's ideas?

If there are no tracks, consider chalking these and taking suggestions from the children about what kind of lines or grids they want. Prompt thinking about double lines, zigzag lines and where these may be seen outdoors.

Planting and growing

Table 2.2 Planting and growing

Possible resources	Potential for mathematical learning
Plant pots of different sizes and shapes	Planting seeds and filling to half full with soil. Adding just enough water with a watering can. Monitoring each day to see whether more water is needed. Recording in children's own way.
Seed trays	Selecting the correct size of pot, which may be different for different seeds and bulbs.
Seeds and bulbs	
Rakes	
Hoes	Thinking of time now and time ahead. How might the weather or surfaces change tomorrow or next week? Maintaining a weather book to record the seasonal changes with photos, comments and how this has impacted on the environment. This will help in developing skills of cause and effect.
Trowels	
Labels	
Stakes	
Mark making tools	
	Counting how many seeds are being planted. Looking to see whether the packaging tells us how many seeds there are or the weight of all of the seeds. Talking about quantity and the comparison of the whole bag to a few, some and half of the seeds being used. This is an opportunity for rich language about how many, how much left and why they think this.
	Patterns on seeds, comparison of different seeds.
	Matching/counting: one seed to each hole or one/two to each pot. How will we know and check that they all have the same number.
	Measuring to make holes the same space apart. Measuring how tall our plants have grown. Posing questions of how we will know how much they have grown.
	Time: thinking about how long it will take the plants to grow.
	Volume: how much water do they need? What is the best jug or can with which to water the plants?
	Estimating/predicting which plant will grow the tallest.
	Comparing: are the plants the same height?

(handwritten annotation: Number bonds to 20)

Photo 2.6 I wonder which is growing more.

Photo 2.7 What's happening in the growing area today?

Photo 2.8 What's happening in the growing area today?

Water investigations

Table 2.3 Water investigations

Possible resources	Potential for mathematical learning
Watering cans Sprays	Free exploration with buckets, funnels, sieves, measuring jugs, different sizes of bottles, containers, cups, tea pots, jugs.
Hoses	Filling and pouring, investigating when full, nearly full, emptying.
Piping	Working out how many cups of water to fill the big bucket.
Guttering Buckets and containers of different sizes	Attaching hoses to the outdoor tap to fill larger containers, covering a larger area. Investigating the length of tubing and relating this to how long it takes to empty and for water to go through it.
Scoops Funnels	Using a builders' tray in which to fill, pour, empty from one container to another discovering the properties of the volume of containers and thinking about conservation of volume, e.g. a tall, narrow container may hold the same amount as a short, wide container.
Jugs Tea pot Water wheel	Using the water wall to make choices about what to measure and with what resources. Children leading the mathematical thinking and planning and perhaps involving other children along the way.
	Exploring floating and sinking, and offering opportunities through careful selection of free choice materials for problem solving, e.g. objects that look heavy but are not, smaller objects that are heavy.

Photo 2.9 What can we explore with the jugs and bottles?

Photo 2.10 How can you get the water from…?

Sand investigations

Table 2.4 Sand investigations

Possible resources	Potential for mathematical learning
Rakes	Selecting buckets, spades and scoops of different sizes.
Buckets	Considering the use of a pop up tent with sand inside. What could this become?
Pop up tent with sand inside	
Combs	Exploring time by seeing how long it takes for sand to run through the sieves/sand wheels.
Spoons and scoops	
Cake tins	Investigating the properties of wet and dry sand.
Moulds	Making patterns with combs, feathers, moulds and seeing a print being made.
Feathers, stones, sticks	Linking the print of a 3D object, e.g. cylinder, with its 2D shape (a circle). Investigating with other objects and regular/irregular shapes.
Imaginative play materials	

Large block play investigations

Table 2.5 Large block play investigations

Possible resources	Potential for mathematical learning
Hollow, large blocks of different shapes and sizes	Selecting blocks needed for their own building plans. Problem solving what is needed for own purposes. Comparing size of models and making opportunities for language of order in context of what is needed within the play and why. Making choices, trying out, reviewing and evaluating.
Large boxes, crates or pallets	Investigating the way in which the blocks can stack and developing children's understanding of how this affects size and direction.
Numbers, mark making materials	Using language of up, down, across, longer, taller, wider.
Measure box with tape measures, trundle wheel, metre stick, ribbons, rulers, sticks	Selecting materials from other areas to bring to the play for their own reasons, e.g. loose parts which fit their reasoning and purpose.
	Natural stepping stones lead to children physically manipulating to put them out and move along, counting. Developing spatial awareness and links with counting by comparing who is further along a line, further away, near to the end.
Community play wooden blocks	Encouraging one to one correspondence.
Stepping stones, logs, tree stumps	Problem solving through their building play by exploring what balances, what fits, what is the best size, measuring.
	Building walls and enclosures: estimating (How many do you think will fit?), counting (How many bricks do you think we need?), exploring height (About how high is our wall? How high can we make it?), shaping (What is the best way to place the bricks to make a strong wall? Which side is most stable?), exploring possible patterns needed when building.

Mud kitchen

Table 2.6 Mud kitchen maths

Possible resources	Potential for mathematical learning
Different sizes and shapes of spoons, bowls, buckets, pots, pans, plates, scoops, tubs, forks, spades, jugs, baking trays and tins, ladles, sieves, plastic bottles, colander, straws, sticks, shells, tongs, scales, whisks	Conservation of volume and capacity through investigation of what to do, make, create and select the tools with which to make it happen. Act out and role play using mathematical language in context: Do you have enough? Do you need more? How much more do we need? Is there a 'cake' in every part of the cake tin?
Metal, wooden and plastic tools	Developing thinking skills and reasoning through filling, emptying, sharing, adding water and changing consistency and noticing the differences in substance.
Wooden pestle and mortar	Developing the concept of more / less/ enough / not enough leading to talking about quantity or comparisons of amount.
Materials to mix: leaves, gravel, pebbles	Sorting utensils according to their functions and being creative in using tools for different purposes.
Scales for weighing	Moving and transporting, making decisions about how to carry, where to carry, the difficulties in carrying something too heavy.
'Recipe' books	Developing possibility thinking and asking 'What if....?' or 'I wonder what could happen...?' questions.
	Sequencing and ordering, making comparisons and using mathematical language to describe what they have found out.
	Developing symbolic play using resources to represent something else. This strengthens children's ability to visualise and abstract as a key stage in later mathematical understanding.
	If children have a range of containers to transport water, mud, stones, sand, bark they learn about weight. How heavy a tin of sand is compared with a tin of stones. Using spoons, scoops, counting how many of each it takes to fill. Observing the changes in consistencies. Using sequencing vocabulary: first I will get a tin, next a spoon, then some sand and finally water.
	Measuring/capacity, positional language, size, considering how many spoons do you need to fill a container, children making chocolate mousse and describing how many spoons, etc. they need, problem solving to get water from the water butt to the mud kitchen.
	Variety of tubs, spoons, ladles, buckets, silicone cake cases, jugs. The mud kitchen affords the children the opportunity to explore without having to worry about mess!

Making mud pies only

Photo 2.11 Maths in the mud kitchen

Den building

Table 2.7 Den building

Possible resources	Potential for mathematical learning
Crates, large boxes Different fabrics, covers, waterproof cushions, twigs, branches, fastening materials, pegs, rope, tape Clipboards, tape measure	Creating the space needed for the purpose of the den. Needing more / less or a different space Consideration of how long it will be there and protection from weather. Making decisions about what to build, how to build, what is needed. Following or giving instructions. Thinking through a plan and evaluating whether it is working. Using positional language to talk about inside, outside, back, front, near to, on top of, how high, how wide. How many children can fit inside? Can an adult get in too? Developing the spatial awareness of shape and size within the space created. How can the space be organised? What is the best way to fit in what children want inside? How can the den be made bigger, wider, taller if it needs to be?

Photo 2.12 How can we build a den?

Thinking zone

A thinking zone could also provide a quiet spot for thinking something through, catching an idea, wondering what next, reflecting.

Points for reflection and discussion

1   How do we provide opportunities for the children to explore mathematially out-doors in such a way that they are motivated to want to learn, revisit, apply and become creative in their thinking and in developing their own ideas?

2   Do we create an atmosphere where exploration and 'having a go' are seen as just as important as getting a correct answer?

3   Do we provide a rich and interesting environment and plenty of experiences where there will be lots of opportunities for problem solving to be embedded as an approach in developing early mathematical awareness and in children developing confidence?

4   Look again at the 12 features of a quality mathematical environment outdoors, and discuss other ways to take each feature forward.

5   Using the tables in this chapter, try to think of some more resources or mathematical ideas that may arise from the children's play.

References

Pound, L. (2008) *Thinking and Learning about Mathematics in the Early Years.* London. Routledge.

Scottish Government (2014) *Building the Ambition: National Practice Guidance on Early Learning and Childcare, Children and Young People (Scotland) Act 2014.* Edinburgh. APS Group Scotland.

Walsh, G. and Gardner, J. (2005) 'Assessing the Quality of Early Years Learning Environments.' *Early Childhood Research and Practice*: Volume 7. Issue 1.

Welsh Government (2014) *Further Steps Outdoors: Guidance.* Cardiff, Wales. Department for Education and Skills.

3 | What knowledge, skills and understanding are children developing through their play outdoors?

Look, I've got the car to fit under. If you put it under the yellow car, it fits. I have built it up so it's the best in the whole world. I put some bricks together and put them up. I will put the car through the big tunnel. It goes into it.

—A nursery child

This chapter will focus on the progression of each aspect of early maths and link it to outdoor learning opportunities. It will also examine the skills, processes and dispositions to learning which underpin effective early mathematical learning, as well as discuss how these can be taken forward in practical ways.

> **Scenario:** While children were gathering sticks to build a fire in the forest area, the following conversation took place:
>
> Child 1: I found these three, I need them this big. (shows the size with hands)
>
> Child 2: Here's a wee stick.
>
> Child 3: We need some more big and small sticks.
>
> Child 1: Whoever finds a big stick, I can help break it into small.
>
> Child 3: We have lots and lots of sticks now. A hundred of them.
>
> Child 2: I think we have enough.
>
> Child 3: You halved that stick into two?
>
> Child 1: We need to make another square.
>
> Adult: How many sticks will we need to make the square?
>
> Child 2: Three, no, no, it's four ones, look.
>
> Adult: What will happen to the popcorn over the fire?
>
> Child 1: It will grow.

Child 2: It will grow bigger and pop out.

Child 3: It will go pop.

Adult: How many pops?

Child 3: 1, 2, 3, 4, 5, 6, 7, 8, 9, 10, 13, 17, 19, 14, 55, 51.

The joy of early counting for a real purpose in children's investigations

This chapter starts by looking at what is happening around the UK and at similarities and differences in the foci for early mathematical development. There are differences in:

- terminology, e.g. Foundation Stage (England, Northern Ireland), Foundation Phase (Wales) and Early Level (Scotland);

- the age range within each of the UK countries for each early years' curriculum;

- the compulsory school age for children starting at nursery and school. There are also differences internationally in starting ages.

This makes it even more important to focus on what provides a really strong foundation for early development upon which children can build into the primary school years. This book places great emphasis on how children learn and make sense in the outdoor environment, but there also has to be a focus on the key conceptual understanding that they need to be building and developing through play.

The Welsh Curriculum (2015) emphasises the importance of children thinking across the curriculum using the processes of planning, doing and reporting on what they have been learning to help develop a depth in learning. The processes of planning, developing and reflecting should be interchangeable. The Foundation Phase is strongly based in maths being developed through oral, practical and play-based activities, engaging in practical tasks, using ICT, and real-life experiences.

The Foundation Phase pedagogy would place emphasis on children developing their mathematical understanding through a curriculum where all of the areas of learning complement each other in both the indoor and outdoor environments. The document further exemplifies the different types of play in which children will be involved and the range of planned activities to include child-initiated experiences. It promotes children as independent thinkers and learners, develops creativity and encourages challenges that inspire problem solving and discussion. Developing mathematical reasoning is highlighted, as well as applying skills to play, selecting appropriate resources and using mathematical language to talk about their own choices and ideas. Children are also encouraged to present their findings in a variety of ways.

The curriculum for early maths in Northern Ireland (CCEA) aims to promote children's thinking skills and personal capabilities across the curriculum and Foundation Stage.

It also highlights the need to develop children's curiosity and interest in the world around them, promoting positive attitudes and dispositions to learning. The Northern Ireland curriculum emphasises the importance of processes in maths, that this should permeate across areas of learning and that children should be able to apply their skills in practical tasks, real-life problems and within maths itself. It also highlights the importance of children thinking and talking mathematically, with skills in logical reasoning, problem solving, creativity and developing thinking in abstract ways.

In England the revised Mathematics in the Foundation Stage (2014) focuses on two learning goals – one for numbers and one for shape, space and measures. In the previous version there was an emphasis on problem solving, reasoning and numeracy. This has now changed to mathematics, perhaps recognising that problem solving permeates all areas of learning. The stages of development in early counting are not so explicit, and for this we can turn to the document Development Matters in the Early Years Foundation Stage (EYFS, 2012), the non-statutory guidance material to support practitioners in implementing the statutory requirements of the EYFS. This provides development stages in children's early mathematical development. The early maths curriculum is also further supported by the Characteristics of Effective Learning as discussed in Chapter 1.

In Scotland, Curriculum for Excellence sets out 14 experiences and outcomes with the suggested 'National Numeracy and Mathematics Progression Framework' on the National Improvement Hub website (Education Scotland, 2016a). Many early years' settings and local authorities have worked on their own development of progression using the experiences and outcomes in a variety of ways, and my own work has been very heavily involved in looking at the underpinning concepts, skills and understanding from birth to five years. Building the Ambition (Scottish Government, 2014) sets out the more general guidance on what quality experiences, environment and the role of the adult should look like in practice, and this is clearly linked with sound pedagogy to the indicators for inspection (Education Scotland, 2016b). I have collated in Table 3.1 what each of the UK curricula identify as key learning in early mathematical development. In a time when governments are looking to raise attainment and achievement in numeracy and maths, it is a crucial aspect of our commitment to young children that we build a shared understanding of the complexities of early mathematical processes and support them in their early learning in a way that is meaningful. In the left-hand column of Table 3.1, I have written the headings as what I would determine to be key concepts as each curriculum describes aspects of maths in different ways.

Table 3.1 Comparison of mathematics at the early stages across the UK

Key aspects of early mathematical development	Curriculum for Excellence (Scotland) Experiences and outcomes, Early Level: by the end of Primary 1 (3–5 years)	Early Years Foundation Stage (England) (3–5 years)	Northern Ireland Curriculum Foundation Stage (4–6 years)	Wales Curriculum Mathematical Development 3–7 Nursery/Reception (R)
Counting leading into number sense	I am developing a sense of size and amount by observing, exploring, using and communicating with others about things in the world around me. I have explored numbers, understanding that they represent quantities, and I can use them to count, create sequences and describe order. I use practical materials and can 'count on and back' to help me to understand addition and subtraction, recording my ideas and solutions in different ways. I can share out a group of items by making smaller groups and can split a whole object into smaller parts.	**30–50 months** Uses some number names and number language spontaneously. Uses some number names accurately in play. Recites numbers in order to 10. Knows that numbers identify how many objects are in a set. Beginning to represent numbers using fingers, marks on paper or pictures. Sometimes matches numeral and quantity correctly. Shows curiosity about numbers by offering comments or asking questions. Compares two groups of objects, saying when they have the same number.	**Understanding number** Count a variety of objects. Develop an understanding of one-to-one correspondence and come to appreciate that the size of a set is given by the last number in the count. Investigate different ways of making sets for a given number within 5/10. Match numerals to sets. Order numerals and sets within 5/10. Develop an understanding of conservation of number within 5/10. Understand in counting activities that 'none' is represented by zero. Explore ordinal number. Explore the number that comes after, before, between a given number.	**Using number skills** Listen to and join in rhymes, songs and games that have a mathematical theme. (**R:** recite a range of number rhymes and songs) Realise that anything can be counted, e.g. claps, steps Count reliably up to 5 objects (**R:** 10 objects) Recite numbers from 0–10 forwards and backwards using songs and rhymes (**R:** 0–20 and from different starting points) Recognise numbers 0–5 and relate a number 0–5 to its respective quantity (**R:** read and write numbers to at least 10) Use mark making to represent numbers in play activities that can be interpreted and explained. Compare and order numbers to at least 5 (to 10)

Shows an interest in number problems.

Separates a group of three or four objects in different ways, beginning to recognise that the total is still the same.

Shows an interest in numerals in the environment.

Shows an interest in representing numbers.

Realises not only objects, but anything can be counted, including steps, claps or jumps.

40–60 months

Recognise some numerals of personal significance.

Recognises numerals 1 to 5.

Counts up to 3 or 4 objects by saying one number name for each item.

Counts actions or objects which cannot be moved.

Counts objects to 10, and beginning to count beyond 10.

Carry out simple mental calculations.

Extend, when appropriate, understanding of number beyond 10.

Counting and number recognition

Count in the context of number rhymes, jingles and stories.

Count forwards in ones within 5/10 from different starting points.

Count backwards in ones within 5/10 from different starting points.

Recognise numerals up to 5/10.

State, without counting, quantities within 5.

Make a sensible guess of quantities within 10.

Explore numbers relevant to their everyday lives.

Extend, when appropriate, counting in ones and recognition of numbers beyond 10.

Extend activities to include counting in 2s, 5s and 10s.

Demonstrate an understanding of one-to-one correspondence by matching pairs or pictures (**R:** understand that zero means 'none')

R: use number facts up to 5

Count in 2s to 10 and in 10s to 100

Use the terms 'first', 'second', 'third' and 'last' in daily activities and play

R: use ordinal numbers to 10 in daily activities and play

R: begin to read number words

Understand the concept of 'one more' in their play **R:** mentally recall 'one more' of a number within 10

Understand and use the concept of 'one less' in their play **R:** mentally recall 'one less' of a number within 10

R: combine two groups of objects to find out 'how many altogether?'

R: take away objects to find out 'how many are left?'

Use counting to solve simple mathematics problems in everyday play situations **R:** solve simple problems in a practical situation that involve simple addition and subtraction up to 5.

(Continued)

Table 3.1 (Continued)

Key aspects of early mathematical development	Curriculum for Excellence (Scotland) Experiences and outcomes, Early Level: by the end of Primary 1 (3–5 years)	Early Years Foundation Stage (England) (3–5 years)	Northern Ireland Curriculum Foundation Stage (4–6 years)	Wales Curriculum Mathematical Development 3–7 Nursery/Reception (R)
		Counts out up to six objects from a larger group.		**R:** talk about addition and subtraction instructions in play activities.
		Selects the correct numeral to represent 1 to 5, then 1 to 10 objects.		**R:** make a sensible estimate of up to 10 objects that can be checked by counting.
		Counts an irregular arrangement of up to ten objects.		
		Estimates how many objects they can see and checks by counting them.		
		Uses the language of 'more' and 'fewer' to compare two sets of objects.		
		Finds the total number of items in two groups by counting all of them.		
		Says the number that is one more than a given number.		
		Finds one more or one less from a group of up to five objects, then ten objects.		

Shape, position and movement	I enjoy investigating objects and shapes and can sort, describe and be creative with them.	In practical activities and discussion, beginning to use the vocabulary involved in adding and subtracting.
		Records, using marks that they can interpret and explain.
		Begins to identify own mathematical problems based on own interests and fascinations.

Early learning goal

Children count reliably with numbers from one to 20, place them in order and say which number is one more or one less than a given number. Using quantities and objects, they add and subtract two single-digit numbers and count on or back to find the answer. They solve problems, including doubling, halving and sharing.

30–50 months

Shows an interest in shape and space by playing with shapes or making arrangements with objects.

Shape and space

Explore and talk about shapes in the environment.

(Continued)

Table 3.1 (Continued)

Key aspects of early mathematical development	Curriculum for Excellence (Scotland) Experiences and outcomes, Early Level: by the end of Primary 1 (3–5 years)	Early Years Foundation Stage (England) (3–5 years)	Northern Ireland Curriculum Foundation Stage (4–6 years)	Wales Curriculum Mathematical Development 3–7 Nursery/Reception (R)
	In movement, games, and using technology I can use simple directions and describe positions. I have had fun creating a range of symmetrical pictures and patterns using a range of media.	Shows awareness of similarities of shapes in the environment. Uses positional language. Shows interest in shape by sustained construction activity or by talking about shapes or arrangements. Shows interest in shapes in the environment. Uses shapes appropriately for tasks. Beginning to talk about the shapes of everyday objects, e.g. 'round' and 'tall'. **40–60 months** Beginning to use mathematical names for 'solid' 3D shapes and 'flat' 2D shapes, and mathematical terms to describe shapes. Selects a particular named shape.	Build and make models with 3D shapes; create pictures and patterns with 2D shapes; investigate and talk about the properties of shapes. Sort collections of shapes in several ways; describe the arrangements. Describe and name common 3-D and 2-D shapes. Explore body space through different types of movement.	

Explore movement through space during indoor and outdoor play activities.

Understand and use a range of positional words.

Explore movement using programmable devices.

Follow/give directions from/to a partner for simple movements.

Can describe their relative position such as 'behind' or 'next to'.

Orders two or three items by length or height.

Orders two items by weight or capacity.

Uses familiar objects and common shapes to create and recreate patterns and build models.

Uses everyday language related to time.

Beginning to use everyday language related to money.

Orders and sequences familiar events.

Measures short periods of time in simple ways.

Early Learning Goal

Children use everyday language to talk about size, weight, capacity, position, distance, time and money to compare quantities and objects and to solve problems.

(Continued)

Table 3.1 (Continued)

Key aspects of early mathematical development	Curriculum for Excellence (Scotland) Experiences and outcomes, Early Level: by the end of Primary 1 (3–5 years)	Early Years Foundation Stage (England) (3–5 years)	Northern Ireland Curriculum Foundation Stage (4–6 years)	Wales Curriculum Mathematical Development 3–7 Nursery/Reception (R)
		They recognise, create and describe patterns. They explore characteristics of everyday objects and shapes and use mathematical language to describe them.		
Measure	I have experimented with everyday items as units of measure to investigate and compare sizes and amounts in my environment, sharing my findings with others.		**Measures** Compare two objects of different length/weight/capacity/area; understand and use the language of comparison. Order three objects of different length, weight, capacity, area; talk about the ordering using appropriate language. Find an object of similar length, weight, capacity, area; talk about their findings in terms of 'just about the same' length, weight, capacity, area. Begin to explore the notion of conservation of length, weight, capacity in practical situations. Engage in discussion about their observations.	**Using measuring skills** Compare, sort and order two objects in order of size, weight or capacity by direct observation **R:** use direct comparisons with: • Length, height and distance, e.g. longer/short than • Weight/mass e.g. heavier/lighter than • Capacity e.g. holds more/less than • Demonstrate an awareness of prepositions and movement during their own physical activities **R:** use prepositions to describe position.

		Included under measuring skills
Time	I am aware of how routines and events in my world link with times and seasons, and have explored ways to record and display these using clocks, calendars and other methods.	Choose and use, with guidance, non-standard units to measure length/capacity/weight; talk about their work. **Within measures** Sequence two or three familiar events. Talk about significant times on the clock. Compare two intervals of time; talk about their observations in terms of took longer/shorter time; explore time patterns; choose and use, with guidance, non-standard units to measure time; talk about their work.
Pattern	I have spotted and explored patterns in my own and the wider environment and can copy and continue these and create my own patterns.	**Patterns and relationships** Investigate and talk about pattern in the environment. Copy a simple pattern. Continue a simple pattern. Create patterns. Explore pattern in number. Discover the components of numbers within 5/10 by investigating different ways of partitioning sets into subsets practically; talk about the outcomes.

Table 3.1 (Continued)

Key aspects of early mathematical development	Curriculum for Excellence (Scotland) Experiences and outcomes, Early Level: by the end of Primary 1 (3–5 years)	Early Years Foundation Stage (England) (3–5 years)	Northern Ireland Curriculum Foundation Stage (4–6 years)	Wales Curriculum Mathematical Development 3–7 Nursery/Reception (R)
			Understand the concept of addition by combining sets of objects to find 'how many'.	
			Match objects in real contexts.	
			Compare sets by matching objects/counting objects to understand the terms 'more than' less than' 'the same'.	
			Investigate the relationship between addition and subtraction in practical situations.	
			As pupils progress through the Foundation Stage they should be enabled to:	
			Use appropriate mathematical language and symbols.	
			Sort and re-sort materials, recording the outcomes in a variety of ways.	
			Talk about data represented in simple block graphs, tables and diagrams.	
			Understand the conservation of number.	

Count forwards and backwards from different starting points.

Recognise numbers to at least 20.

Carry out mental calculations such as 1 more/less than up to 20, doubles up to 10 and mentally add and subtract within 10.

Understand that 'teen' numbers are made up of 10 plus another number.

Begin to measure using non-standard units.

Talk about the properties of 3-D and 2-D shapes using appropriate mathematical language.

Be involved in solving practical problems.

Understanding money (within number heading)

Use money in various contexts;

Talk about things that they want to spend money on.

Understand the need to pay for goods.

Become familiar with coins in everyday use.

Talk about different ways we can pay for goods.

Demonstrate an awareness of the purpose of money through role play.
R: use 1p, 2p, 5p and 10p coins to pay for items

Money

I am developing my awareness of how money is used and can recognise and use a range of coins.

(Continued)

Table 3.1 (Continued)

Key aspects of early mathematical development	Curriculum for Excellence (Scotland) Experiences and outcomes, Early Level: by the end of Primary 1 (3–5 years)	Early Years Foundation Stage (England) (3–5 years)	Northern Ireland Curriculum Foundation Stage (4–6 years)	Wales Curriculum Mathematical Development 3–7 Nursery/Reception (R)
Information handling	I can collect objects and ask questions to gather information, organising and displaying my findings in different ways.		Use their number skills in shopping activities.	
	I can match objects, and sort using my own and others' criteria, sharing my ideas with others.		**Sorting**	
			Explore freely properties of a range of materials and one/two/three property collections; respond to questions about the arrangements.	
	I can use the signs and charts around me for information, helping me plan and make choices and decisions in my daily life.		Sort collections of random materials.	
			Sort for one criterion using one-property materials; talk about the arrangement.	
			Sort for one criterion using two-property collections; re-sort for the second criterion; explain their work.	
			Sort for one criterion using three/four-property collections; find the various possibilities; explain their work.	
			Partition sets into subsets in preparation for exploring components of number.	

What are some of the underpinning skills that permeate across all areas of learning but require mathematical focus? These will be revisited in different ways throughout the book but an initial list may include:

- noticing similarities and differences (things that are the same and not the same)
- reasoning (what belongs to a set, what does not belong and why)
- visualising (e.g. Can you close your eyes and think of how far the number track is going to reach?)
- predicting (e.g. What would happen if I add one more bead to the string on the fence?)
- mark making (children's own mathematical representations of their thinking and their ideas)
- asking questions
- communicating their ideas and suggestions in a variety of ways
- refining and evaluating (e.g. How could I use the bricks to build a bigger tower?)
- comparing (more/less, longer/shorter)
- estimating (e.g. How many more are needed?)
- sorting (for their own criteria and in creative ways, to show what belongs/does not belong to a set and justifying why they have sorted in different ways).

Developing early mathematical awareness takes time and is a complex process with an interrelated set of skills and conceptual understanding which need to be explored, revisited and applied in different contexts. This makes the outdoor environment an ideal setting for new experiences and making connections with those developed in the indoor setting, and vice versa. Children also learn at their own pace, making sense and meaning in very different ways of how they see the world, the level of maturity they bring to the planned experience or child-led experiences and their previous experiences from the home setting.

Within whatever curriculum you are working, learning mathematically in the early years is not a linear process. We need to appreciate that children will revisit concepts at a different and deeper level as they gain in confidence and experience. *Heinemann Active Maths at the Early Level* (Keith and Mosley, 2012) identifies three levels through which young children will develop their conceptual understanding, and this, in turn, can help with how we plan to meet the needs of each child. The first is a stage of early understanding during which they play at a purely exploratory stage, developing their curiosity through a very practical and active way. In the outdoors, children would be investigating what resources are there, how they can be used, how to navigate the bike through a space and how to recognise numbers simply as labels for the purpose of their play. Confidence grows when they can build on this understanding, make links, learn more from each other and play mathematically in a more cooperative way. In the second stage, they will begin to see a greater purpose for mark making as their symbols take on more meaning, even if at this stage it is just to themselves. The final stage is extending understanding where children are beginning to test out new ideas, apply skills and prior knowledge in different contexts, beginning to talk about their learning in a more coherent way, especially in describing their initial plans and in evaluating how they worked or did not work out and how they solved problems. The role of adults in scaffolding these stages of confidence, understanding and independence in learning is crucial to young children's mathematical development, and this role will be explored in Chapter 4 in more detail.

In the next section, I will explore the main aspects in which children will be mathematically involved, list mathematical terms that they will be meeting in this new language and suggest some key stages in the development of mathematical awareness to support thinking about the experiences we can plan to support this early mathematical learning.

Early counting, leading to developing number sense and using adding and subtraction

Opportunities for mathematical language

- more, less, enough, not enough, too much, too little, none, nothing, zero
- the same, nearly the same, not the same, match, pair
- one, two, three, etc.
- before, after, between, next, last, middle, order
- count, count on, first, second, third
- and, add, add on, join, put together, altogether, total, how many
- makes, is the same as, balances
- remove, take away, hide, how many left?
- split, share, fair, each, same amount
- half, halve, double, near double.

Key stages of development

Acknowledging the importance of children's understanding of numbers as labels before they move onto quantities

Early mathematical learners can relate to the number 3 or 4 as this is often their age. Children relate to numbers in the environment for the purposes of their play and this is not necessarily about counting quantities. This has to be encouraged in the outdoor environment with plenty of opportunities for children to have or create their own number labels, to number car park spaces or simply talk about the numbers all around them on an outdoor walk in the wider environment of the street, park or shops.

Very young children can recognise small quantities, often 1, 2 or 3. They can relate this to picking up objects and holding one object in each hand. Young children enjoy talking about 'big numbers' without a real understanding of quantity. They will recite numbers in rhymes and songs and have the motivation to join in especially with props to help make the links between numbers and quantities. When we plan for individual children outdoors we need to be aware of the sensitivities in using a more direct 'how many is that?' question as it may take away the sheer enjoyment of exploration of numbers.

The **counting principles** of Gellman and Gallistel (1978) have been well documented and provide us with a sound basis for assessing children's ability to count with understanding. This needs to be shared by all staff working with young children in their mathematical development and with parents and carers in family learning to fully appreciate the need to take counting at children's pace and recognise these vital stages of development. When children count they need to have experiences in the following.

One to one counting

This involves the ability to count each object only once, to touch, count and physically move an object before having the skills to touch and count and finally to be able to remember which objects have been counted and which have still to be counted. We need to consider which resources in the outdoor environment promotes this stage of counting: by moving the tyres one at a time, stacking the blocks to make the tower, moving the balls along a string on the wall to see how many there are. Real contexts for counting that arise from the children's natural curiosity and desire to count will impact greatly on their attitudes to seeing a purpose in counting. At this stage, children may not count in the exact order but may still recognise that you give each object a 'count' number.

Stable order principle

At this stage and through the embedded experiences of rhymes and songs, children will recognise the order within our number system at least within smaller quantities to 10. The 'teen' numbers can still provide difficulty as 11 and 12 are just words, but when children hear 13, they often hear the familiarity of a sound similar to three but do not recognise that the number begins with one. The developmental stage of place value and pattern in our number system takes time, but we can assist in this process by providing children with ground number tracks, indicating through sparkly lights or a star on '10' why this is an important place. Children at a later stage of development will recognise that 11 is one more than 10 and begin to see pattern as well as developing the links between place value and spatial awareness. See Chapter 5 for the developmental stages in number tracks.

Cardinal principle

When children count out stones, pebbles, etc., we are likely to find that they:

- count without counting each item individually (child may need more experience in count, touch and move)
- count all of the objects, then, when asked, tell you something completely different to the overall quantity, e.g. there are 6 stones but the child counts to 8 (the child may need more experience in count, touch and move by physically putting each pebble as they count it into the bucket)
- count all of the stones correctly, then, when asked how many, count them all again and keep repeating this. In many cases this is simply because children do not understand that the last number you count tells you how many there are altogether. This needs to be talked through in a child-like way, e.g. making the last stone 'magic' with a wand on it and asking the child to catch this last number and hold in in their head. This concept takes time, especially with larger quantities, but without revisiting with a supportive adult, many children will often continue to count all, and even in their addition they will not be able to count from a given number as they can't yet fully appreciate the importance of the final number to be counted.

Abstraction principle

This involves children in moving from counting objects that are the same (5 cars) to an understanding that if we choose 5 different objects to count (a twig, a stone, a pebble, a shell and a fir cone), this is still 5. In other words, the abstraction principle develops the concept that anything can be counted.

The Order irrelevance principle

We need to provide children with plenty of experiences to practise and understand the concept that it does not matter where you start counting, the overall final count stays the same. You can develop this by rearranging items with the children, e.g. how they have placed a line of pebbles, and asking, 'I wonder if you still have 5? Can you move them around another way and check? Can you put them in a circle and see whether there are still 5 altogether?'. This is a strong indication of the child's understanding of the conservation of the quantity of 5 – that is, it can be arranged in a variety of different ways.

With this strong foundation in early counting, children can build on concepts of addition and subtraction by combining quantities to find out how many there are altogether. This can be further investigated by providing opportunities for children to count on 1 more, 2 more, then 1 less, 2 less.

In children's play, encourage sharing by starting with a whole amount and providing some small tubs for children to match one to one and develop the earliest concepts of division by sharing. Everyday contexts of sharing tools in the outdoor environment will also offer real opportunities to investigate sharing. The extension of this concept will be to investigate putting a large quantity of objects into groups of the same quantity, e.g. 3 seeds in each pot.

Taking the experiences outdoors

- Use the language of '1, 2, 3, go' so that children understand that they have to wait for the final number before running the race. Count back '3, 2, 1' in a similar way to start the obstacle run.

- Select different sizes of buckets and baskets for children to fill, and talk about who has more/less and how they could find out.

- In one nursery, the children had been very interested in the 'Fitbits' the staff were wearing and asked whether they had reached 10,000 steps yet. Staff are trying to source pedometers for the children to use in nursery and at home.

- Sort and match different quantity of objects to photographs. Find context where it would be helpful for children to check that everything is in its correct place.

- Create a ball abacus, with children helping to thread the balls through and deciding on where to put it and how long to make the string.

- Have a magic counting wand outside or a Counting Ted who goes out to help anyone with their outdoor counting.

- Take the rhymes and songs outside, and make up some new rhymes to fit the outdoor setting, e.g. '5 little buckets were on the wall (and 1 had a great big fall)!' Create an outdoor rhyme book with the children.

- Provide lots of mark making tools for children to represent their own marks and symbols.

- Have some outdoor picture or photo cards to show one or more of the same object on each card (e.g. 1 tyre, 2 tyres, 3 tyres). Use the washing line for children to explore and add to this experience. Mix the cards and let children choose what else could be photographed for the place on the washing line where there are 3 objects.

- Play and join where appropriate with children's own counting games on chalked grids or lines. Encourage them to mark make to keep the score.
- Set a 'counting challenge of the week' to find a different hidden number of objects in the outdoor environment.

Scenario: Two children were talking about what was needed to make cakes in the mud kitchen.

Adult: I wonder what we need to make the cakes?

Child 1: Oh, lots, lots and lots.

Adult: Anything else?

Child 1: Water. [She fills a jug.] Look, half a water.

Child 2: I need more flour.

Adult: I think that the recipe book inside says we need four scoops to make cakes with the playdough. So do you think it will it be the same for the mud cakes?

Child 2: Put more than four in. The mud is bigger.

Measuring

Opportunities for mathematical language

- more, less, enough, not enough, too much, too little
- the same, nearly the same, just over/under
- full, empty, half full, holds, fits, covers
- heavy, heavier, heaviest, light, tall, short, long, wide, narrow, thick, thin, fat, big, small
- balance, measure, weigh, pour, fill, compare.

Scenario: A nursery child was building a bed for himself, and once completed, he counted the bricks in order to 12. He asked an adult to lie down to make her bed and measured alongside her. He said that his bed was too short; it needed to be taller for her. He added more bricks and asked the adult to try it out. 'It's just right', he said, counting the bricks up to 16. The adult then expressed concern that the bed wasn't wide enough, so the child said he would add more at the side for her arms.

Key stages of development

Children begin to measure the space around them as they play and investigate outdoors. They begin by using their own words to depict the measure, often depicting everything as 'big', whether talking about length or weight. It is important that we model the correct term without taking away from the fact that this early stage of measure is needed. The context of the outdoors is real in giving purpose to the experience as children can then use their measuring experiences for real purposes, e.g. which spade is better to dig a big hole in the sand? At the next stage of development, children will order and compare big, bigger, biggest, and it is often useful if the buckets or spades are ordered on a bench or hung up in order of size with a shadowed cutout behind to match the outline and shape of the bucket. This gives children a better choice from which to make a decision, rather than all of the resources being mixed up together and causing frustration when something can't be found.

Taking the experiences outdoors

- Collect tools to create a measuring box, using the children's suggestions about what would be useful to measure different objects in the outdoor environment, e.g. ribbons, metre sticks, rulers and measuring tapes for length. Store these in a central place for easy access.

- Add in a spirit level to motivate children to make comparisons and to check whether models and building creations are straight.

- Use different contexts for measure by providing large footprints for measuring, large containers for weight and different sizes of fabric to cover the ground and gain experiences first hand of covering an area.

- Let children explore a set of weighing scales outdoors – even if they are not at the stage of reading scales, they will 'act out' the weighing experience through their play.

- Investigate pulleys in the sand or water trays. Let children work out how to move something to where they want it.

- Hide different sizes of sticks and let children work together to put them in order of smallest to biggest.

- Develop the conservation of length by providing different lengths of string, rope and ribbon and change its shape when placed in a box.

- Set up investigations with willow sticks and let the children find out what or who is taller – the stick or a child.

- Decide with the children what is the best size of guttering for outdoors. Record their decisions and how they are using it in different play situations.

- Explore the mud kitchen, enabling the children to have access to a variety of equipment.

Photo 3.1 Which holds more?

Photo 3.2 Can you put the potatoes in order of size?

- Set out some den building materials and step back to observe the many measuring skills children will have to apply for their own purposes.
- Develop a 'maths outdoor measure book' for all of the findings and recording of investigations through photos, children's comments or their own mark making and symbols.

Pattern

Opportunities for mathematical language

- spotty, dotty, zigzag, etc.
- after, before, between, next, last, match, start, finish
- repeat, over and over, grow, round and round, circle, line.

Key stages of development

Children's earliest experiences of pattern are those in the wider environment where they can explore long before understanding the definition of something that follows a given rule. We tend to rush children to the more formal aspects of copying and completing patterns before they have fully investigated what is natural in pattern making. Children use the word pattern in a general way to describe a picture that has been made and to talk about pattern on their clothes, on animal patterns and in rhymes and songs.

Children need to investigate a variety of pattern making: linear patterns going horizontally and vertically, growing patterns as they build with blocks creating staircases, cyclical patterns going round and round and linking days of the week and months and seasons as a cyclical pattern.

All of this is necessary to help children gain a feel for maths, as patterns are fundamental to maths relationship links and connections. Through their play we can build the vocabulary of 'first, next, then'. There are strong links between pattern and sorting as children look for similarities and differences and make decisions. Pound (2008) uses the term 'pattern seekers', and this sense of curiosity is at the heart of maths and in making connections.

Taking the experiences outdoors

This earliest stage of pattern development is crucial for children's understanding about the way in which the environment is organised and develop a sense of order.

- Go on a pattern hunt in the outdoors environment to find patterns in nature and in the resources with which children are working.
- Investigate the different wellies on a fence to look at different patterns, and start from children's own terminology for these – spotty, wavy, dotty, pointy, stripes, etc.

Table 3.2 Developing pattern across learning areas indoors and outside

Maths area/display	Outdoors	Malleable area	Snack area	Poems and stories
Pegs and pegboards	Collecting objects with patterns or some which will print a pattern.	Dough/plasticene/clay patterns using a variety of mark making materials	Visual recipes	*Elmer*
Beads and laces			Decorating cakes	*Pants*
Buttons			Making fruit kebabs	*Aliens Love Underpants*
Sorting materials	Natural objects			Adapting *We're Going on a Bear Hunt*
Grids	Outdoor pattern book – photos of patterns in the environment			'I can make a pattern'
Mosaic tiles				
Magnetic/velcro pictures				
Visual timetables	Obstacle course			
Days of the week displayed in a circle to show the cyclical nature of time	Tyre prints / Bunting			

Imaginative play	Construction	Sand and water	Creative area	ICT
Patterns in home corner	Bricks and blocks	Making patterns with sticks, rakes, combs, shells, stones, feathers, prints.	Painting, printing, drawing	Software patterns
Washing line	Growing patterns		Cutting and sticking	Clip art
Different fabrics		Creating patterns in water	Collage of fabric/wallpaper patterns	
Design centre:			Making wrapping paper, hats – real contexts for creating a pattern	
Wallpaper, materials, ribbons, shopping bags, clothes				
Clothes shop				

- Explore the patterns that tyres leave when going through mud or water, or footprints in the sand, as boots, shoes and wellies come out of puddles, or patterns as children dig in the mud.
- Look for patterns on crates or on walls, and enhance the play with magnifying glasses and binoculars.
- Children can design their own obstacle course or extended play with crates as they decide what to put first, then next.
- Create a 'patterns everywhere' outdoor book to include photographs of the patterns the children have found.
- Make links to children investigating patterns they can find at home and encourage them to bring these into the early years' setting to share through display or include in a big book.

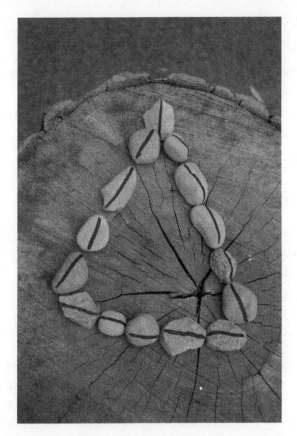

Photo 3.3 Making a 'pattern'

Photo 3.4 Extending the pattern

- Create 'patterns' with chalk, squirty water bottles, paint brushes of various widths on different surfaces.
- Select objects from nature and in the surroundings to create a 3D picture.

Early money

Opportunities for mathematical language

- cash, coins, penny, pound, change
- spend, how much?
- ways to pay, value, too much, just right
- card, cash machine.

Key stages of development

Play is essential in the earliest stages to develop the concept of exchange – children need experiences to buy something and get items in return. They may hand over a bundle of coins with no sense of cost and value. Children then begin to be aware of different ways to pay, cash and cards, and they talk about money as it naturally arises in play situations. The outdoor environment offers a new context outwith the playroom shop. Different shopping experiences may be developed, and extended contexts can be explored where money may be used, e.g. getting on the bus, paying for the cakes made in the mud kitchen, entry to the game/obstacle course they've created. Real experiences of shopping with cash are also important as children have limited experience of seeing money being handed over in exchange for goods. It is equally important for children to be aware of online shopping and to involve them in talking about and watching the ordering process happen.

Taking the experiences outdoors

- Children may use stones, pebbles to represent money as well as resourcing with coins, notes, cards, purses, shopping bags, tickets
- Digging for coins or to look for treasure
- Paying to get on the train or bus, or at the garage for petrol

Information handling

Opportunities for mathematical language

- sort, match, same, not the same, does not match, belongs, does not belong, because, if…then

- together, label, chart, ask, most, least, fewest
- find out, show, display, answer
- sign, symbol, information, read, plan, help, make, design.

Scenario: Let's talk about rainfall

This investigation started with the question from children asking how much rain falls from the sky.

Child 1: We could count the rain. Splash in puddles to see how much rain comes out.

Adult: How could we catch the rain?

Child 1: In a bucket.

Adult: What else could we use a bucket for?

Child 2: Washing a car. Holding in the rain.

Adult: How could we stop people tripping over the bucket?

Child 1: Put it in the ground.

Adult: Someone might put their foot in the bucket.

Child 2: Put something on top. Make a sign to say 'Look out!'

Children then designed containers to collect the rain. They looked at various jugs and other containers, and the talk inevitably led to a discussion about why they had lines on them – to show how much water was in the jug. Children then devised their own calibration levels and started taking photographs after each rainfall to monitor the amount of rain.

Key stages of development

Children's innate curiosity leads naturally to sorting and organising resources and objects in ways that make sense to them. We need to encourage children to talk about why they have put different things together in a way that makes sense to them so that sorting experiences do not heavily rely on sorting for colours, shapes and textures. In the outdoors, the scope for sorting for their own criteria is greatly extended, as will be the language and reasons for sorting. Through their play they will bring together materials that serve the purpose for where the play is leading, e.g. 'I need something to make a wall', and in this way they are developing key skills in looking for similarities and differences in the features and properties of objects in a much closer and refined way than simple experiences can offer with limited properties inherent in the resources. In this way they are making decisions about what goes where and why it goes there, justifying the features or properties that make it belong to a group or set of similar objects holding the same property. It is helpful to think of this key learning as developing an awareness of a 'something-ness'. This could be function, e.g. good for building and stacking, good for joining and connecting a large construction, could help in creating a water construction. These experiences for sorting lead to a greater level of thinking skills through quality play. How children gather information and record their findings should also provide choice in the selection of how this may be done.

In many situations the sorting leads directly into the play, and at other times, children may find the need to record more formally on a Venn diagram or a Carroll diagram. The sorting becomes more organised in its display by recording the criteria for being sorted, e.g. on the left-hand side of the diagram, sticks, and on the other side, objects that are not sticks. The ability to discriminate between something that is and is not supports children in their mathematical thinking in a more challenging way than simply sorting out into colours to make a set of red, blue or green. Therefore, the wide ranges of both experiences and ways for children to record findings as they choose is crucial in helping them make sense of the information. Recording tools, such as mark making resources, clipboards and different types of paper including grids and squared paper, need to be on hand.

Curriculum for Excellence includes an outcome not specifically highlighted in other curricula for early mathematical awareness, and this is the link to children creating and using signs: '*I can use the signs and charts around me for information, helping me to make choices and decisions in my daily life*' (Education Scotland, 2010). The scope for creating their own signs, deciding on why children need a sign, what it is for and what it says provides a natural link to early literacy development. Play links learning across all areas, and what we may think of as mathematical or literacy based is simply play to a child. These implicit links build a strong foundation for the application of skill and confidence in learning without the division of 'subject' areas in the child's mind.

Taking the experiences outdoors

- Going on a sound walk or pattern hunt. (What can you hear; what can you see? The train, or birds? Record the results.)
- Going on a mini-beast hunt (record information on what the children found).
- Providing opportunities for children to match and sort different natural materials – leaves, stones, loose parts – and sort these in their own ways and for their own purposes.

- Voting on games to make outside.
- Using sticky notes to record their favourite activity outside and compiling these to create a pictorial graph.

Shape, position and movement

Opportunities for mathematical language

- same, not the same
- build, stack/does not stack, rolls/does not roll
- match, face, flat shapes, objects, pointed, round, corner, side, print
- in front, behind, beside, on top, under, inside, outside, off
- forwards, backwards, straight on.

Key stages of development

- Proximity (how close things are)
- Putting things together and pulling them apart, constructing and deconstructing
- Rearranging things in space, changing objects around, position, locality, perspective, different viewpoints
- Directions moving forwards, backwards, turning but not necessarily the language of left and right
- Links to inside and outside a space
- Discovering where can things go in space (how to get them there, working around obstacles in the way)
- Simple properties of objects: sorting what rolls, joins, fits, goes beside, thickness
- Exploring different shapes to develop an understanding that they have different properties/features for comparison.
- Asking, 'What can you do with it? What can you make? How can you combine? What do you need to add to it to make…?'
- Varying heights and levels to develop an awareness of perspective and positional language
- The outdoors offers different shapes and objects to investigate, move, turn, fill, place with different textures, and different properties for sorting for its use (What does it do? What can I do with it? What can it become? How can I join it with something else? What's best to make a…?)

Taking the experiences outdoors

3D to 2D links

- Making an imprint: footprints, prints with all sorts of natural objects in compost or sand, tyre tracks or prints on paper (these are rich experiences which will lead to more formal 2D shapes when children see the print being made)
- Asking, 'What can we fit in the flower pots? How much space will they take up?'
- General moving around in a wide space and having to negotiate the space in a different way
- Helping to design an area gives way to children having to project and visualise things in space, drawing up plans, reviewing designs, looking at photos
- Using a selection of large blocks to create their own constructions, obstacle courses and as symbols in their play, e.g. a large block as a mountain (through this play we can observe the skills they are using, the decisions they make and how they interact with these larger resources outdoors)
- Going on shape walks and explorations
- Making large constructions and taking photographs of creations from different angles
- Using bikes, scooters and wheeled toys for positional language
- Den building to make decisions about what will go on top or on the ground and what fits inside
- Looking for the right objects and shapes to fit, fill, drop, throw
- Creating maps and using programmable toys to give directions.

Time

Opportunities for mathematical language

- today, yesterday, tomorrow, now, later
- soon, earlier, later, next, last, how long?
- day, morning, afternoon, night
- quick, slow, fast, days, weeks, months, seasons
- timetable, clock, calendar.

Key stages of development

In some curricula, time is linked logically as another way to measure. Time is very subjective for the young child and in a similar way to number, they will often relate time to special times of the day or time that are meaningful to them. There can be few practitioners who have not been asked 'Is it home time yet?', and without a very simple and child-appropriate answer, this can lead to responses like 'soon' or 'in a little while', which means very little to the curious or upset child. Young children need to hear the words for time in a context that makes sense, and often with pictures, to support this learning of order of time. If this very abstract concept is presented to children using the vocabulary of ordering the events in a personal way, for example, 'When we came into the nursery today we…now you are…then it will be…and then it will be home time', it gives children a much clearer indication of where each section of the day is in relation to each other. This fundamental understanding of how young children make sense of time can, therefore, be applied in the outdoors by talking with children in their planning about what they may do first, next, then, or in reviewing with the children how they made something.

The seasonal changes and changes in weather are all first-hand experiences in outdoor settings. They also offer the mathematical links with which clothes are worn for which purposes and when, which activities can be carried out and why or why not depending on the time of year.

Duration of time – how long something takes – is a key opportunity for outdoor learning in maths with very real contexts for understanding. By using a timer, children can make sense of the fairness of taking turns for the bikes, how many balls they can throw into a big box in 10 seconds or how long it takes to empty the water tray. This sense of time, balanced with children's understanding that there are different ways to measure the time, is as vital as developing understanding of the telling of the time using a clock which is an entirely different skill.

Taking the experiences outdoors

- Making clocks using hoops, twigs for hands
- Taking seasonal walks and observing and recording seasonal changes
- Following routine or sequence cards for getting outdoor clothes on and off
- Turn taking with bikes or a climbing frame to develop a sense of time.

Problem solving and play

> To solve problems children and adults alike have to draw on their experiences of the world. The younger the child, the less experience they will have to draw on, which is why it is important to give them problems that allow them the freedom to investigate without any feeling of failure.
>
> *Mathematical Development* (Welsh Government, 2008)

Problem solving is central to developing an investigative approach through a range of mathematical experiences.

Case studies

Building a den for 'Bob the Gnome'

In the woods it started to rain, and the children decided that Bob needed a shelter. We explored the den-building box for a suitable piece of material. It had to be 'nice and big' to cover Bob and 'maybe the fairies if they come to visit'. A waterproof tarp was selected, and then children began to discuss how to make the cover stay up. They decided to attach it to the trees, and then we had to find pegs to clip it on – the little pegs were 'too small' and 'not strong enough' so we used the 'big yellow pegs'. Staff then asked the children 'how many' we would need. Children counted these out and began to peg the tarpaulin in place. The tarpaulin sagged in the middle, so staff asked the children what we could do to hold it up. There was lots of discussion about rope and how we would attach it. The staff member stood under and poked it up with her hand; some boys said, 'We could use something to hold it up inside'. Staff members asked if there was anything in the woods we could use – 'sticks'. Children went in search of sticks and brought various ones back to try. There was lots of very good chat about length of sticks and comparing, and then they decided they needed a 'bigger stick'. The stick was found but was not long enough to hold the roof 'high', so one boy found a tree stump to put under the stick to 'make it longer'. One of the girls asked where the fairies would sit if they came to visit (there are fairies and fairy doors hidden throughout the area). We counted the fairies and then found small pieces of wood and stumps so all the fairies would have a place to sit if they visited. The children then proceeded to bring branches/leaves and twigs to decorate Bob's Den.

Transporting tree stumps

Some trees had been cut down in the garden and cut into large stumps. We gave the children the task of transporting these to the wild wood. Initially, the children tried to lift them but they were too heavy. Staff questioned children to think what they could use to help move the stumps. One boy said, 'We could use that bucket'. A staff member said that it might still be too heavy to carry and asked whether there was anything else in the garden that had handles that they might be able to use. Children suggested 'the wheelbarrows' and 'the bike with the trailer on the back'. Children fetched the wheelbarrows and trailer and proceeded to try to load the stumps on. There was lots of discussion about the size of the stumps and whether they were 'too big' to fit. Children still struggled to lift them, so the staff member asked them to look at the shape and wondered (out loud) if there was an easier way to load it on. Children said, 'Turn it on its side…we can roll it!' Discussion followed of the circle shape and how it would roll one way but not another. Stumps were loaded and children worked together to push them to the wild wood area, but then hit a snag when they got to the stairs. They wondered what we could do now. It was too heavy to pull the wheelbarrow and the stump up the stairs. 'We could try rope' – discussion followed about how long and thick the rope would need to be. 'Could we roll it up?' 'All together.' Children proceeded to roll the stumps up the stairs, load them back into the barrows and get them to the wild woods.

Bridge

The children at Corsehill EYC, Kilwinning, were trying to make a path across the water 'full of sharks and crocodiles'. There was much discussion about the length of the wooden planks required to go between the tyres and crates they were using to create a 'bridge'. Conversations followed about how heavy the boys were and how strong and thick the planks of wood were, as the first boy tried to make his way across the shark- and crocodile-infested water, and the plank started to bend. They also negotiated that each person would have a turn. There was lots of chat about who would be first, second and third and it went on to just giving numbers in order, i.e. 1, 2, 3, 4. The adult noted that this was an opportunity to introduce some ordinal numbers to their vocabulary. They tried planks of wood side by side, trying two overlapping planks before opting for two planks tied together. They were already familiar with using cable ties in creating areas in the outdoor area and opted for this solution with only a little support from adults.

Number drop zones

The children at Corsehill EYC were creating a maths area outdoors. They were making a drop zone where the children could play a game alone or with adult support. Through this experience, children were recognising numbers by dropping the matching quantity of balls down the tubes.

Staff tried to follow the children's ideas as much as possible. There was a lot of discussion about which number should go first, and children were quite insistent that because 1 came first it had to be the biggest tube. As with everything created with the children and in following their ideas, it worked really well, and children were able to continue making up their own games and transferring their skills to other areas and materials.

Photo 3.5 Drop zones

Here are some prompts that may further promote children's problems solving and investigations outdoors:

- Can we make a bird feeder?
- How could you use all of the different sizes of spoons in the bag?
- Can you find some patterns on the mixed up socks on the washing line?
- What do we need to make a mini garden?
- Which numbers chalked on the wall can you hit with the water bottle?
- Let's hunt the numbers.

- What numbers can you make with the sticks?
- Follow the footprints outside.
- Can we make an obstacle course?
- How can we make a car park?
- Let's make a game with the buckets and balls.
- What goes through the hoops?
- Can we make a number book with things we found outside?
- How far can you throw/how high can you throw?
- What information do we need for creating labels outside?
- Can you thread the ribbons through the fence to make a pattern?
- How long does it take?
- Let's go fly a kite.
- What can we find to make some shakers?
- Let's write some numbers on wood/with chalk, etc.
- Where can we find numbers/patterns all around us?

Points for reflection and discussion

1   What do you notice about the different ways in which early maths is represented in each curriculum design?
2   What ideas can you take from this chapter to motivate children in their mathematical learning?
3   How would you set up a new problem for children to investigate or respond to children who want to find out something?

References

Department for Education (2014) *Statutory Framework for the Early Years Foundation Stage: Setting the Standards for Learning, Development and Care for Children from Birth to Five*. London: DfE.

Education Scotland (2010) *Curriculum for Excellence: Numeracy and Mathematics Experiences and Outcomes*. Available at www.education.gov.uk.

Education Scotland (2016) 'National Numeracy and Mathematics Progression Framework'. National Improvement Hub. Available at http://education.gov.scot.

Education Scotland (2016) 'How Good is Our Early Learning and Childcare?' National Improvement Hub. Available at: https://education.gov.scot/improvement/Pages/frwk1hgioearlyyears.aspx.

Gelman, R. and Gallistel, C. (1978) *The Child's Understanding of Number*. Cambridge, MA. Harvard Press.

Keith, L. and Mosley, F. (2012) *Planning and Progression Guide: Heinemann Active Maths Early Level*. London. Pearson Education Limited.

Pound, L. (2008) *Thinking and Learning about Mathematics in the Early Years*. London. Routledge.

Scottish Government (2014) *Building the Ambition: National Practice Guidance on Early Learning and Childcare, Children and Young People (Scotland) Act 2014*. Edinburgh. APS Group Scotland.

Welsh Government (2008) *Mathematical Development*. Cardiff. Welsh Assembly Government.

How can we support young children in their learning?

The role of the adult is fundamental in taking children's learning forward. In doing so, we need to respect the child's learning journey and use our observations well to know when to sustain and share the thinking, take forward and promote new ideas for the child and, most importantly, draw upon our own knowledge of progression in skill development.

In this chapter, the focus is on using questions as starting points for investigations and helping support children in planning, reviewing and evaluating their learning through mathematical conversations. Links will be made and exemplified with recent developments in mark making to show how children's learning can be shared and recorded in a variety of ways. The focus on creativity in mark making for children's own purposes will also be explored as they make meaning from their own experiences.

The guidance offered in *Building the Ambition* (Scottish Government, 2014) illustrates the key messages about our role in engaging young children effectively through the headings in 'Experiences which' and 'An environment which is' and 'Adults who', as well as in the discussion of 'Well-being', 'Communication' and 'Promoting curiosity, creativity and inquiry'. In the analysis below, I have taken from the *Building the Ambition* document those points that are most appropriate to show how they relate to early mathematical awareness in particular.

> Adults who:
> Help children make sensible choices about their learning by involving them in making decisions about what could be provided and evaluating their own experiences.
> Provide a range of resources to talk about which encourages children to be creative.

In early mathematical awareness, children need time to explore the environment, try out and explore what they can do with different materials and reflect on what has worked for them in their own way through their mathematical play. Children-sensitive interactions which allow enough freedom to investigate and persevere with their problem solving but not to reach a stage of frustration that may lead to a 'can't-do' attitude. Therefore, the second point is crucial for knowing each child as a mathematical learner, their stage of development in applying skills, in their dispositions to maths and the knowledge they are building in a safe and secure environment.

> Adults who:
> Understand children will start at different points and encourage them to try activities at the appropriate level.
> Make time to talk and listen to what a young child is saying and try to build on their meaning and reply in a way that children will understand but also models new language and descriptions.
> Give time for children to explain their interests in a calm unhurried manner but also elaborate on what the child has said by asking probing questions to further extend the child's use of language.

We need to tune in to each child as an individual and know their interests and how they are learning mathematically. Young children need the time to revisit early mathematical concepts and layer this new learning to build confidence. With someone who is genuinely interested in what they are saying and how they are thinking, children's confidence will grow with a reassurance that there is no one way. This attitude is vital as children progress in maths and often gain the feeling of trying to work out what someone else is looking for rather than how they are seeing the mathematical problem and processes themselves.

> Adults who:
> Help children express ideas by singing, making music and role play.

Through this type of expression, children do not see maths as something different. It becomes an inherent part of everyday life where the number names become more meaningful and connected with the experience of joining in with rhymes and songs. There is scope to make this more focused by creating the children's own maths rhyme books, combining the established rhymes with some that the children will make up or change to suit the interest at the current time. Their own mark making to accompany this takes on a new level of motivation and participation in the learning. The sheer joy of music and creating new songs to familiar tunes also supports their learning in early literacy and rhyming experiences. The links between children's imaginative play and writing are well documented. In *Exploring Writing and Play in the Early Years* (2003), Hall and Robinson demonstrated the wealth of rich language and mark making that arose from the context of Mr Pipe's garage, and, where often we can see obvious links with literacy, perhaps we need to also seek the underpinning mathematical potential that arises naturally from children's play.

Adults who:
Encourage children to try out new things, using children's interest as a starting point.

This big new world of maths can only be enhanced by our own increased knowledge and understanding of how young children learn best. If we fully appreciate that many mathematical concepts are not developed quickly, but require children to consider, reflect, try out, revisit and build on their skills and understanding, then perhaps any gaps in learning may be reduced with a strong foundation at this early stage. Julie Fisher (2016) describes this in her research about quality interaction with a literacy focus, and it is equally true of early mathematical development.

Adults who:
Involve children in making sensible choices about their own learning by helping them to plan and evaluate their own experience.

Sometimes children don't have any plan when they enter the setting and their planning only becomes evident as the play emerges and they start to take it forward. However, if children lack the confidence to think things through or, in talking about what they want to do, the skills of planning may not be observed. We need to look at how children are interacting with their environment as well as what they are doing to help to make sense of how they are learning in different situations. Consider how to make time to talk with children upon entry on a personal level, as well as in welcome group times. The 'setting of the scene for the day' helps to make that link from home to the learning setting and enables us to talk about what is offered in the environment and introduce any new resources or prompts for thinking. The skill in evaluating mathematically is also complex without having an interested adult to talk to. Children require different language to express this, and if this is not modelled in the early years, then we can't assume that a later stage children will automatically have the language of evaluation to discuss what they learned, how they learned and what they plan to do next. Often the simplest technique of giving the child an 'ask me about...' sticker can provide the immediate feedback to a child that the learning in which they are engaged is valuable, and also can prompt you to return to talk with the child at a suitable time of the day. The stickers also help in making a link with home as children can be encouraged to further share with families what they have been doing during the day. In this chapter I will explore the variety of language skills involved in early maths and consider how this new language can be developed. In this way the next important messages within *Building the Ambition* (Scottish Government, 2014) will be discussed.

> Adults who:
> Encourage the young child to think, helping them to solve problems and giving the child time to come to a satisfying conclusion from the child's view and then taking time to discuss this together.
> Give time for children to explain their interests in a calm unhurried manner but also elaborate on what the child has said by asking probing questions to further extend the child's use of language.
> Encourage a young child's learning by suggesting they try things out, inspire curiosity and see that this is essential to how children learn.
> Are not afraid to change their own plans and take the lead from the child and who are able to act as a support to the young child when needed.
> Will admit when they don't know but offer to help to find out together and see this as valuable both for the child and themselves.
> Pose questions which encourage inquiry such as, I wonder if, why do you think that, to extend the young child's ability to verbalise their thoughts and actions.
> Ask children I wonder what happens if…to help children make sense of what happens when you try things out?

Key considerations include how we support children in the problem solving process without interfering and giving solutions but also how we find and make quality time to talk about what they have been doing. It is in these more personal times with a child that the quality of interaction is based critically on our observations so that we can make comments on the what, why and how in a way that does not become a question and answer session but focuses our role as a commentator on the mathematical play. Phrases like 'I was interested in how you…', 'I hadn't thought of doing that…' or 'I was wondering what made you think about…' create a different context for discussing the learning and provide the appropriate language in the right way that is relevant to the particular child's development. David Perkins (2003) emphasises the importance of 'making thinking visible' and this requires the types of environment where talking about your own learning and what you are thinking can encourage children in their dispositions to learning in a positive way.

> Adults who:
> Recognise differences in starting points of the individual child and encourage them at the appropriate level.
> Praise the child's growing physical capabilities and challenge them to take the next step.

Offer different ways and words to children to extend their vocabulary.

Take account of a child's home language and who make every effort to incorporate this into daily conversations.

All children are on a continuum of mathematical development, and it is important that we start from where the child is 'at' and not what they can't do (Bruce, 1987). When children have difficulties in maths in the school years, it can often be attributed to a gap in their developmental stages, lack of experience with a particular concept at a level of depth or the lack of practical engagement with appropriate resources to build up he concepts before moving on to more pictorial representations. In other words, we have to question moving our young children too quickly to concepts that require abstract thinking without the play-based experiences required to make maths more meaningful. If we recognise these different rates of development, but also appreciate that 'the more effective the environment for mathematical learning, the more confidence as practitioners we gain', then we can build on what we know children have the potential to do, given the right circumstances. Throughout this book, we have seen examples of this in practice, as well as the wealth of experience that children may have mathematically if we take time to find out the pictures that lie behind their thinking. It is very true that if we are unsure of maths or had poor experiences ourselves at school, then we tend to rely on what we think early mathematical development should be, rather than consider what it could be, in making a difference to children's later development. In this way, perhaps, we can also develop children's independence, self-assertion and positive self-image (CCEA, 2006), when we know that this is central to children seeing themselves as mathematical learners.

Adults who:

Encourage children to see another's point of view through joint projects and coop-eration in play.

Create opportunities for children to 'write' in different play situations and for different purposes without this being conducted in a formal way.

Encourage children to talk together with their friends and create situations where children take turns and listen in small groups.

Encourage children's ideas, allow them to make mistakes, can offer further sugges-tions and praise their attempts.

Children have the potential to learn from each other in their mathematical play. This was evident in a nursery where staff placed different stages of the washing line resource development in plastic pockets at the children's height level and talked, as they were setting it up, about the first things that children may like to find out about in the first pocket (e.g. pictures of objects to hang on the washing line). Then, in the next pocket, were things the children would have to work out a bit more (e.g. which teddy came after the one before), and, in the pocket at the right-hand side, there were lots of numbers (to match up to the quantities). It was set up in this way to support the shared understanding of staff in the developmental stages, but when they stepped back, they observed that children began working together, drawing on what each knew, to put the quantities in order and pegging the numbers to match the quantities. This is an excellent example of planning an experience with an overall anticipated outcome of children moving through each stage of development which turned out to be children driving their own understanding. This will not happen in all cases with all children, but it is an important point to consider what hooks each individual child into the learning process. Another nursery began chat books to let children informally talk about anything they wanted to talk about in a short small group session and lead the topic for discussion. This has also been adapted to an outdoor maths chat book where children's informal comments, observations, transcripts of their talk, mark making and photos have created another context for children sharing their mathematical ideas.

Adults who:
Help model techniques and strategies with children and encourage this new learning in the child's new challenges or suggest a new context.

Photo 4.1 Maths chat book in the outdoor area

When I am invited into early years' settings and in the primary school to model what I consider to be effective practice in supporting and enhancing children's mathematical learning, I am very conscious that the focus has to be on taking the children's learning forward. It is not uncommon for me, in a nursery setting, to start 'playing' with a resource I have brought in and to 'think aloud' in the hope that a child will come over and ask what I am doing and decide to join in. Some look, some return and some don't visit the experience at all, but many children observe to see whether you are a playful person. Children are highly astute as to the value you give to play and whether it is a serious thing to do. I have often said that to be accepted into a child's play or for children to want to join in and to see you as a co-player is a privilege. It is not uncommon for children to demonstrate attitudes to learning, ways of learning and knowledge of maths through more active or play-based pedagogy in the early (and later) stages of school in a way that may not have been seen in other ways of teaching and learning methodology. The term 'active learning' is not about children running around noisily with lots of resources everywhere. The focus has to be on the deep level of engagement which, given the right circumstances, takes children to a different level in their thinking and motivation for maths.

The value of the quality of interaction, alongside meaningful contexts for learning, is one which has to be shared with parents and carers. We need to consider the family learning opportunities for that extended shared understanding of how young children learn about maths so that they, in turn, can support their own everyday experiences in the home and wider environment.

The Researching Effective Pedagogy in the Early Years (REPEY) study highlighted the importance of sustained shared thinking as a key indicator of quality settings (Siraj-Blatchford et al., 2002). The value of the key ways in which staff can support children through effective questioning was explored, and the definition of 'sustained shared thinking' was given as:

> an episode in which two or more individuals 'work together' in an intellectual way to solve a problem, clarify a concept, evaluate activities, extend a narrative, etc. Both parties must contribute to the thinking and it must develop and extend.

Mathematical language is often thought of simply as terminology, as described in Chapter 3, where the terms we use and how we use these in our interactions can support children in their independent use. Think about how you may use these words at the right time in the right context. Some children will take on board the terminology quickly if they are making the connection between the concept and a link that is important to them, e.g. *this is bigger than that one*, in making a comparison. However, other children may still use their own words to describe their own ways of thinking and development, e.g. *this is lots big and that's teeny*. Just because they are not using the correct terminology does not necessarily mean that children do not give meaning to the experience, but,

..x the language needs to be practised in a range of contexts and with sensitive .o to model the appropriate terms for children to hear. If this is not done, children will call everything 'big' and not differentiate between the measures of tall, heavy, short, etc. Similarly, the more we use thinking language, the more we can encourage children to take it on board as a way of talking about their learning, e.g 'What do you think…?'; 'Why do you think that…?'; 'What makes you think…?'.

Asking questions

Knowing the right question or prompt to give at the right time in the right way to different children takes time, experience and practice to develop. We can have a tendency in early mathematics to give too many closed and highly focused questions, which rely heavily on children's recall and memory skills, e.g. What shape is this? A more open-ended approach would include:

- How would we know that this is a…?
- How could we work out who has more?
- Will there be enough for everyone to have one each?
- How many do you think there will be?
- Can you think of a way to get from…to…?
- Do you think that…?
- How many ways can you…?

Planning language

Planning language helps children to predict, to draw on exisiting knowledge, to think in terms of ordering or sequencing a plan (first, then, next). It may involve children thinking about what they may use to carry out a task. You may ask, for example:

- What do you think would be good to use to build the obstacle course?
- How could we find out how about how to build a garage?
- What will we put in our plan first? Do you have any ideas?
- Can we think of some ideas first, then decide what we can do today?

Using language to explain a process

When encouraging children to use mathematical language to explain a process, you may ask, for example:

- Can you talk me through what you did?
- What made you decide to…?
- How did you know how to…?
- What do you notice when…?
- What did you decide to…?
- Can you explain to the other children…?
- How did you solve the problem?

Language of reflection and evalution

Questions to encourage the use of language of reflection and evaluation may include:

- What did you enjoy in the water today? Why? Have you any other ideas for another time?
- Do we need anything else to join the crates together?
- How can we make it fair for everyone to have a turn?
- What was exciting about outside today?
- Would you do anything differently next time with the…?
- If I wanted to make a…, what do you think I should do?

Prompts to help sustain the mathematical play

Some prompts to help sustain the mathematical play might be:

- What about….
- Would a…help…?
- Could you try…or…?

We can also sustain the engagement by using non-verbal communication strategies – nodding, smiling, etc. – to maintain the child's involvement. In many early years' settings, staff will either have question prompt cards on a key ring or there may be shared prompts on the wall or in each area to maintain a consistent approach to involvement in children's interactions. Children also respond to seeing questions on the wall, as challenges, or Can you…and I wonder how to…prompts to help them in devising their own questions.

The following scenarios show different types of mathematical interactions and conversations in the outdoor environment. Consider which key messages are evident in the dialogue.

Scenario 1: Child-led game arising from investigation

K (a child) was investigating some assorted sea shells and small wicker baskets. She was filling the baskets with small shells. J (an adult) went to play alongside her and began to put shells into a basket too. K tipped hers out and counted them.

K: I got 12. How many have you got?

J: I've got 10 shells.

K: That's back from 12, I won.

(They repeated the process.)

K: How many now?

J: I've got 14 this time, how many do you have?

K: 17. I went past your number, so I won.

(They repeated the process again.)

K: Who won? I got 28.

J: I've got 18.

K: I did, I did. I went further than you.

(They repeated the process again. K had 26, and J had 34.)

K: You winned this time 'cause you got more than me.

Scenario 2: Quality interaction supporting children's well-being

The adult introduced children to a box full of balls of different sizes. As the children investigated these, they commented on them.

Children: 'This one is really heavy.'

'I like this shape – it's squidgy.'

'This one is really big, and this one is tiny.'

The adult then asked: I wonder if all the balls will roll?
(The children proceeded to experiment with the various balls to see how they would roll.)

Adult: Does the big ball roll much further? I wonder how far the heavy ball will roll?

Children: 'This one goes really far.'

            'I'm going to roll this one really hard to make it go far.'

The adult then encouraged the children to try rolling the balls down a slope to see whether this made them go further or faster. Children were commenting on speed and distance. A metre stick was introduced to provide a challenge for the more able children to 'measure' distance. The quality of the interaction came from the open-ended nature of the questioning and from allowing the children to engage and explore the materials in an active way through play – the activity was not dominated and directed by the adult, but children were encouraged to explore and investigate.

Julie Fisher (2016) discusses the importance of finding the right balance between adult-led or -initiated and child-led conversations, as well as the need to listen more and intervene less. If we wait to be asked into a conversation, we can then build on the children's interests in driving forward the dialogue. To be able to tune into the child's thinking, in a way that the conversation becomes more shared and less directed by the adult, requires good knowledge of each child and knowing the level of interactions which will keep the momentum going.

Williams (2008) also highlights the need for high-level discussion and describes key features of effective early years' mathematical pedagogy as the need for practitioners 'to support, challenge and extend children's thinking and learning through sustained shared thinking and use of accurate mathematical language'. He also identified the need for young children to have opportunities to record their understanding and thoughts in early mathematical mark making.

Why mark making in maths?

The work of Hughes (1986) and Carruthers and Worthington (2006) has been instrumental in raising awareness of the value of children's mark making, the developmental stages to look for and how we can gain an insight into children's thinking. Through their marks, children are communicating their ideas, expressing their feelings, developing imagination and creativity, and testing their hypotheses about the world. These opportunities for 'making thinking visible' are fundamental to children's learning and development and should be the entitlement of every child. At the heart of this research lies the child's ability to choose how to represent their own thinking and create their own meanings in their own way with graphics and layouts devised in their own way. This key experience provides a developmentally appropriate way for children to make sense through their own symbolic representations before symbols for maths and numeracy are introduced more formally. Children will draw upon their own experiences to create their own scribbles, drawings, numerals and signs, and in writing will show the influences of standard symbols and tally marks and will use them in contexts that require mark making for their own play purposes. Engaging with this research enables us to observe more closely how children are mark making in a similar way to early mark making in early literacy, but with a taxonomy of stages of development which is highly powerful in building children's confidence in talking about and representing maths in a deeper way. This is a key foundation for later success in mathematics, with implications for sustainability and progression in the primary school as children explore more mental methodology and are still making sense of the world of maths.

Photo 4.2 Stages of development: measuring to mark making to record how tall

Scenario: A child had gone to part of the garden on his own and was drawing lines on a fence post. He told the adult that it is a 'measuring stick'. She measured him, and then he measured her and discussed who was taller. He then worked independently, looking around the garden for different items to measure, like planks of wood and bricks. He was absorbed in this activity for around 30 minutes.

Scenario: In the nursery, a small group of children were beginning to develop their understanding that number symbols represented quantities and explored this through matching in a seed planting activity. Children then went on to predict how much soil it would take to fill the flower beds.

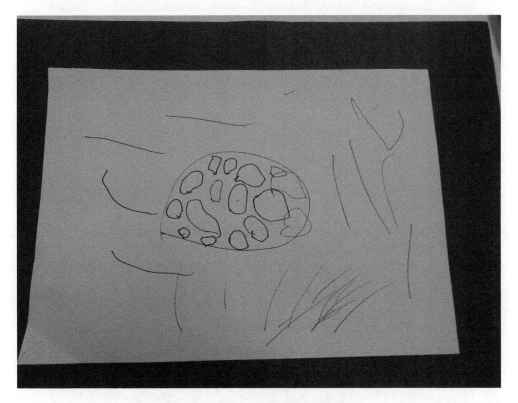

Photo 4.3 How much soil will it take?

Photo 4.4 Transferring the information into tally marks

Photo 4.5 The sensory garden design

They worked in pairs to test out their predictions counting the numbers of wheelbarrow loads it actually took. As each barrow load was emptied into the flower bed the children crossed off one of the marks on their invented prediction mark making representation. They then counted how many wheelbarrow loads and transferred their marks into a sheet of tally marks to show the representation of quantities.

Finally, they took their mark making into the creative design of the garden.

Case study

Isla's wedding cake

Isla had been walking around the outdoor area, clearly making decisions about what she wanted to do next. She rummaged through a box of various fabrics and chose one long piece, then proceeded to wrap it around herself like a scarf. She approached the early years' practitioner (Louise) and me, and said 'I'm going to a wedding.'

'Have a lovely time,' we said, and she went off, chatting to some other children playing nearby. Five minutes later, she returned to us and asked, 'Will you draw me a wedding cake?' Several children were already mark making with large chalk on the ground. 'I'm not sure how to draw one,' I said and, turning to Louise, I asked, 'Do you know how to draw a wedding cake?' Isla then intervened. 'I'll help you. My mum makes wedding cakes. You need three cakes: a big one, then a smaller one and a really small one on top.' Louise took the chalk, and the following conversation ensued:

Louise: So how do I start?

Isla: It needs a really big cake at the bottom.

Louise: Why can't it go at the top?

Isla: 'Cos it's the biggest.

Louise: Ah, so that will be the first layer.

(Louise drew the outline of a large cake on the ground.)

Isla: That's good, but now you need another on top, but it needs to be a bit smaller.

(Louise followed Isla's instructions.)

Louise: OK?

Isla: Now the top cake. It's the smallest.

           (Louise completed the outline of the top layer of the cake.)

Louise: So, what happens now?

Isla: We'll decorate it.

           (She called in some other children and asked if they wanted to help.)

Isla: I'll draw the people at the top, and you could do flowers if you want.

           (At this point we stood back from the drawing.)

Louise: Can I take a photo of what it looks like before you start decorating it so that we can see what it looks like now and then when you finish?

Ten minutes later the children had collaborated and worked individually on the decoration, adding chalked ribbons and 'patterns' until all were satisfied and stood back to admire the drawing that they had created.

Photo 4.6 The bottom layer of the cake on some plates

At this point a child on a bike approached the 'cake', oblivious to the importance that Isla had placed on its creation.

Isla: Stop! You nearly squashed the cake!

Louise: I think that you might need a sign.

Isla: We'll put these round it.

          (She showed her friends what to do, and vertical marks were added to protect the cake.)

Isla: That means don't squash the cake.

Louise: So when is the wedding?

Isla: It's today, soon.

Photo 4.7 The vertical marks mean don't touch the cake!

Louise: Well, what about a sign beside it to tell everyone in case they want to come?

(Louise picked up the chalk and asked Isla whether she wanted to draw the sign.)

Isla: No, you do it.

Louise: OK, but I'll need some information.

(She talked through Isla's ideas, confirming what she wanted on the sign.)

Isla: Let's get ready for the wedding.

The play continued with children acting out the wedding scenario.

Discussion points

1   What added to the quality of the dialogue?

2   How did Louise and I sustain Isla's thinking through the process?

3   Isla initially chose to ignore Louise's suggestion of a sign but has an obvious interest in and understanding of signs. Instead of being a co-player, what steps could Louise plan to take Isla's mark making forward?

4   What particular mathematical skills were evident in this play scenario?

5   Isla brought a lot of her own experience to this play episode. How can we ensure that we have an understanding of children's interests from home to enable us to tap into mathematical possibilities in the early years' setting?

I posed the question about what makes quality interaction to practitioners who had been on my courses and subsequently tried to think in different ways about what made quality interaction in early maths. The following comments show how they took ideas forward to develop quality and sensitive intervention:

- quality of the engagement of children in discussion
- genuine interest in what children bring to the session
- knowledge of the progression in aspects of maths to plan for possible lines of development
- quality of the questioning and prompting – both verbal and non-verbal – which is specifically targeted to the child/group in an open-ended way
- encouragement of a growth mindset and positive dispositions, with praise when necessary and feedback on the processes and achievements being demonstrated by the child.

Points for reflection and discussion

1 How can we develop more shared sustained thinking with children to develop maths conversations?

2 How can we develop our own questioning techniques and have a shared understanding of key prompts for thinking?

3 How can we further the importance of mark making in children's mathematical play?

References

Bruce, T. (1987) *Early Childhood Education*. Kent. Hodder and Stoughton.

Carruthers, E. and Worthington, M. (2006) *Children's Mathematics: Making Marks, Making Meaning* (2nd edition). London. Sage Publications Ltd.

Carruthers, E. and Worthington, M. (2011) *Understanding Children's Mathematical Graphics: Beginnings in Play*. London. Open University Press.

Council for the Curriculum, Examinations and Assessment (CCEA) (2006) *Understanding the Foundation Stage*. Belfast. Early Years Interboard Group.

Department for Children, Schools and Families (DCSF) (2008) *Mark Making Matters: Young Children Making Meaning in all Areas of Learning and Development*. Nottingham. DCSF Publications.

Fisher, J. (2016) *Interacting or Interfering? Improving Quality Interactions in the Early Years*. London. Open University Press.

Hall, N. and Robinson, A. (2003) *Exploring Writing and Play in the Early Years* (2nd edition). London. Routledge.

Hughes, M. (1986) *Children and Number*. Buckinghamshire. Blackwell Publishing.

Perkins, D. N. (2003) *Making Thinking Visible New Horizons for Learning*. Available from http://www.newhorizons.org/strategies/thinking/perkins.htm.

Scottish Government (2014) *Building the Ambition: National Practice Guidance on Early Learning and Childcare, Children and Young People (Scotland) Act 2014*. Edinburgh. APS Group Scotland.

Siraj-Blatchford, I., Sylva, K., Muttock, S., Gilden, R. and Bell, D. (2002) *Researching Effective Pedagogy in the Early Years (REPEY)*. DfES Research Report 365. HMSO London. Queen's Printer.

Williams, P. (2008) *Independent Review of Mathematics Teaching in Early Years Settings and Primary Schools*. Final Report. Nottingham. DCSF Publications.

What resources can support and enhance mathematical learning outdoors?

The bus is going to Blackpool and London. It is £1 to get to Pakistan. The coffee in the café is expensive. They don't even sell juice! The pirate hat is £5. How many do you want? Five? They are cheaper tomorrow. Two pence.

—At the role play bus station

The key resource will always be the interconnectedness of the child, the adult and the environment in which the learning takes place. However, every outdoor area will be different and this chapter will outline a range of contexts for learning and the potential of a variety of resources looking at what children may see, what they may say and how we can take this forward. It will also explore how to challenge children in their mathematical learning outdoors. Some imaginative play areas take on a very different focus in the outdoors and in the resources that can be used so this chapter will focus on possible contexts which lend themselves to quality play opportunities to develop children's mathematical thinking and enable them to build upon key early conceptual understanding. Children become very engaged in their learning when they can independently find resources to use in their play.

In this chapter, different contexts for learning mathematically outdoors will be explored. This discussion may inform a staff member in their interactions in many contexts, such as:

- everyday contexts outdoors, e.g. going to the shops
- focused outdoor contexts, e.g. 'Where can we find numbers?'
- play area context, e.g. 'Let's make a car wash.'
- taking rhymes and songs, e.g. *The Wheels on the Bus*, and storybooks, e.g 'We're going on a pattern hunt' (*We're Going on a Bear Hunt* by Michael Rosen) outdoors

- outdoor bags and boxes, e.g. 'What can we measure today?'
- number tracks and washing lines, e.g. 'What can we find out about counting and numbers?'

Number tracks and washing lines will also be explored as key resources outdoors to develop early counting skills and provide the experiential learning necessary for later visualisation of abstract number concepts.

Many of the resources in this chapter may not be thought of as conventionally mathematical. However, it is the maths that can be drawn from the resources, where and how the resources can be used flexibly and stored, and how children interact with them that helps them to make mathematical links and to connect in a creative way. Ginsberg (2006) concludes that the object and events are not themselves mathematical but afford mathematical thinking.

The following tables outline the potential of these different contexts for learning by suggesting possible key skills and building on the discussion in Chapter 4 – prompts to support children in their thinking and sustained mathematical conversations. At the end of the chapter you will find a blank table for new contexts that may arise in your work with the children, and this may be a helpful tool to record children's learning, their comments or suggestions about the context and your evaluation of the context along with further possibilities to revisit it at a later stage.

Table 5.1 Large boxes

Context for learning: large boxes	Key skills in mathematical thinking	Possible prompts for thinking
Selection of different sizes of cardboard boxes and large tubs and crates Some large cardboard boxes that can open and close or can be flattened Boxes that can fit inside each other	Matching Comparing Sorting Sequencing/ordering Noticing the same/not the same Measuring Making choices Problem solving and refining ideas Predicting	What types of boxes are there? What are they for? What can you make with the boxes? What can you put inside them? Do any of the boxes fit inside each other? What would be a good box for...? How could we make the boxes stronger if they keep falling down?

Table 5.2 Can you make a game?

Context for learning: Can you make a game?	Key skills in mathematical thinking	Possible prompts for thinking
Skittle sets (small and large)	Deciding and making choices	What kind of game can you make?
Balls of various sizes	Predicting	What could we use the big skittle for?
Dice (1 to 6 dots; 1 dot and 2 dots; numbers; blank to write on)	Reasoning	Who will we give a medal to? Why?
	Refining ideas	What could we use the cubes for?
Notepad and pen/ whiteboard and markers	Creating	How can you win the game?
	Planning	What if someone scores…?
Number label cards	Counting	Is there another way to play the game?
Medals	Designing	What else would you need?
Chalked grids, lines, tracks, circles within circles	Measuring	How many can play?
	Problem solving	Are there rules to the game?
Large carpet squares	Evaluating	What would help you score high/ win/get there first?
Bean bags, hoops, quoits, cones, tunnels, planks		
Resources for keeping score: grids, paper		

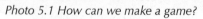

Photo 5.1 How can we make a game?

Photo 5.2 Can we make an obstacle course?

Table 5.3 What can you make with the chairs?

Context for learning: What can we make with the chairs?	Key skills in mathematical thinking	Possible prompts for thinking
Chairs from the indoor area, a big chair, stools or tree stumps Microphone Camera Video recording tool Number cards, sticky notes Pallet as possible 'stage' or platform Fabric, access to dressing-up clothes	Matching Comparing Sorting Sequencing/ordering Noticing same/not the same Measuring Predicting Reasoning	What could we use these to make? How could we sort the chairs? How can we arrange the chairs? Will there be enough chairs for everyone? How can we find out? Will everyone need a chair? What can we use the camera for?

Table 5.4 Teddy bears' picnic

Context for learning: Teddy bears' picnic	Key skills in mathematical thinking	Possible prompts for thinking
Variety of teddy bears of different sizes Plates, cups, bowls, table cover, straws (not all of the same quantity) Pencils/notepad/ notebooks	Sorting Matching Predicting Reasoning Comparing Planning Counting Imagining Sharing Selecting resources	What do we need for the bears? What could we use for food? How will we know what the bears want to eat? What would happen if more bears arrive? How will we know whether there is enough? How can we make it fair for each bear? What else do we need? What will happen if it rains?

Table 5.5 Builders' yard

Context for learning: Builders' yard	Key skills in mathematical thinking	Possible prompts for thinking
Builders' tray	Sorting	What is being built in the yard today?
Logs	Matching	Where are you taking things to?
Bricks/blocks/planks	Predicting	How will you get there?
Tyres	Reasoning	Do you have enough?
Hard hats	Comparing	Do you need anything else?
Shovels	Planning	When does the yard open/close? How do we know?
Planks	Counting	
Signs	Measuring	What jobs do people do here?
'Office' resources	Sharing	
Mark making materials	Selecting resources	

Photo 5.3 What's happening in the builders' yard today?

Table 5.6 Music wall

Context for learning: Music wall	Key skills in mathematical thinking	Possible prompts for thinking
Cheerleader shakers and pompoms	Sorting	What's the best instrument to make a…sound?
Twirling ribbons	Matching	Are there any instruments we need to make? How can we make them?
Bells and musical instruments home made/bought	Predicting	
	Reasoning	
Pots, pans, shakers, spoons	Comparing	Do we have enough of each instrument?
Musical notation paper	Planning	
Picture labels of instruments to follow the music cards as a score	Counting	Do we need anything else?
	Sharing	Are you thinking of putting on a show for us? Can you think of a plan for this?
	Selecting resources	
Laminated sheet music	Making decisions	
	Ordering	What time will it take place? How will we know?

Photo 5.4 What sounds can we make?

Table 5.7 Transient art

Context for learning: Transient art	Key skills in mathematical thinking	Possible prompts for thinking
Everyday resources in the outdoors: twigs, stone, leaves, etc. Paper, cardboard cut in different shapes and sizes, paper plates, fabric in different lengths and shapes; napkins	Making decisions Sorting Matching Predicting Reasoning Comparing Planning Counting Sharing Selecting resources Evaluating	I like the way you… That's an interesting object to choose to put on… What are you thinking of now? Can we take a photo to share your ideas with others? What do you like best about your 'picture'?

Photo 5.5 Creating with transient art

Table 5.8 How can you make some big bubbles?

Context for learning: How can you make some big bubbles?	Key skills in mathematical thinking	Possible prompts for thinking
Washing-up liquid	Sorting	I wonder what we have to think about to make some big bubbles?
Large water tray	Matching	
Whisks	Predicting	What do you need?
Spoons	Reasoning	Do you think that this will take a long time?
Hose piping	Comparing	
Cones	Planning	How do you think you can make the water more bubbly?
Buckets	Counting	
Frame of a splatter pad for pan or bubble making frame	Imagining	
	Sharing	How many bubbles do you think there are?
	Selecting resources	

Photo 5.6 How can we make some big bubbles?

Table 5.9 Let's build a car park/car wash for the cars

Context for learning: Let's build a car park/ car wash for the cars	Key skills in mathematical thinking	Possible prompts for thinking
Wheeled toy vehicles	Sorting	How many cars can you fit in?
Buckets, different sized sponges, cloths, sponge gloves	Measuring	How can you work it out?
	Predicting	What might be best to clean the cars with? Why?
	Reasoning	
Signs created by children	Comparing	How will you get the cars to dry? How long do you think this will take?
Mark making tools	Planning	
Chalk for creating lines	Counting	What signs do you need? Why?
Long and short brushes	Imagining	What will happen if a big lorry comes in?
Keys	Sharing	
	Selecting resources	What's the best sponge to wash...?
	Handling information	
	Recording	Which sponge do you think holds the most water?
		What could we also offer to wash?
		How much does it cost to park the car?
		When does it open/close?

Consider the use of different weather boxes for rainy, foggy, sunny or snowy days to take outside and help children link seasonal events and changes with their understanding of time. The Outdoor Learning page on the Leicestershire County Council website has an extensive list of examples for each of these (Leicestershire County Council, 2017).

Taking rhymes, stories and songs outdoors

Number rhymes and songs have always played a key part in the mathematical experiences of young children. The links with stories which have a mathematical focus or lend themselves to mathematical conversations has been well documented (Keith and Mosley, 2012; Stevens, 2008).

The pictorial clues in stories also help children in developing understanding with very concrete material to more abstract thinking. Therefore, stories can provide a strong visual context for remembering and for children to talk mathematically and make links with their own lives and experiences. As many stories involve problem solving, the richness of our questioning can provide a context for children to become involved in predicting and in asking questions. The repetitive nature of rhymes, and in some stories and dialogue, also assists in helping children to hear patterns within a story. There is potential for our stories to be taken outside, and in so doing, to develop their language by using mathematical terms in context. In addition, children can also be encouraged to create their own stories. By providing a story creating box with appropriate props, they will apply knowledge of story structures and characterisation within their play. Their knowledge of place and setting can also be enhanced through the outdoor environment. *We're Going on a Bear Hunt* by Michael Rosen could easily be adapted to a pattern hunt, shape hunt, number hunt, treasure hunt. Think about the potential of stories which have a focus on:

- Money
    - *Teddybears Go Shopping* by Suzanna Gretz
    - *The Shopping Basket* by John Burningham
    - *The Great Pet Sale* by Mick Inkpen

- Time
    - *Peace at Last* by Jill Murphy
    - *What's the Time, Little Wolf?* by Ian Whybrow and Tony Ross
    - *Clocks and More Clocks by Pat Hutchins*

- Measure
    - *Dear Zoo* by Rod Campbell
    - *Someone Bigger* by Jonathan Emmett and Adrian Reynolds
    - *You'll Soon Grow into Them, Titch* by Pat Hutchins

- Sorting
    - *Dinosaurs Love Underpants* by Claire Freedman and Ben Cort
    - *Harry and the Dinosaurs* by Ian Whybrow and Tony Ross
    - *Jumblebum* by Chae Strathie and Ben Cort

- Number and counting
    - *Handa's Surprise* by Eileen Brown
    - *Kipper's Toy Box* by Mick Inkpen
    - *Wibbly Pig Has 10 Balloons* by Mick Inkpen.

Photo 5.7 The story creating area

Photo 5.8 The Three Billy Goats Gruff and anyone else?

Many of the traditional and well used rhymes for counting back and on are always supported by the props to add to the level of engagement, but this is also necessary in the association of the rhyme and action during it when quantities change. The more visual the rhyme, the more children will remember the order and sequence of both the rhyme and numbers within it.

As with story creation, there is a strong place for making up our own rhymes with the children. Often personalisation gives greater attachment to the rhyme if the child's name is in it. The following words can be set to the tune of *Mulberry Bush* and can give focus to the skills we are planning to develop.

- How can we sort the shells in the tub (x3)
- To see what we can see?

- What can we make with the…today? (x3)
- …and how can we make it?

- What did Lynda make today? (x3)
- Let's ask her how she made it.

- What can we plan to build today? (x3)
- And what will you use to make it?

- What can we measure outside today? (x3)
- And what is best to measure?

- What patterns can we see in the (mud/water/puddles, etc.) today? (x3)
- And tell me what do they look like?

There are many resources that will be part of the continuous provision within the outdoor environment, i.e. those that are always there as part of the planning for a given time. Staff will add to these resources in response to interaction with children and in taking on board children's own ideas and suggestions to provide the stimulus for new mathematical learning.

Continuous provision may also include:

Table 5.10 Resources for continuous provision

Outdoor measure box	Mark making and recording tools	Shopping
Rulers, metre stick, trundle wheel	Large chalks, crayons	Baskets, bags, purses, money, cash register, cardboard ATM, price labels, receipts, price tags, notepads
Ribbons, string, lollipop sticks, sticks for varying lengths	Paint brushes of different sizes and thicknesses and buckets of water	
	Decorating rollers	
Tools for measuring rainfall: bottles calibrated in different ways	Clipboards, laminated sheets	**Programmable toys**
	Squirty bottles, sprays	Direction cards
	Long rolls of wallpaper	Arrow cards
	Whiteboards and pens	Programmable toy grid to create paths, tracks or grids
	2cm and 3cm squared paper	
	Walkietalkies	
	Talking tins	
Timing	**Loose parts centre/store**	**Coverings**
Sand timers (hourglasses)	Shells, pebbles, twigs, sticks, stones, fir cones	Plastic sheeting
Stopwatch	Guttering	Bubble wrap
Timetables (for cars, buses, etc.)	Crates, pallets	Fabric
	Joining materials: masking tape, string, pegs	Table cloths
Thermometer		Flags
	Cable drums	Cushions
	Jumbo tweezers	Pop-up tent
	Pipes, ropes	
	Bamboo canes, trellis	
	Large nuts and bolts	
Small world imaginative resources	**Collecting tools**	**Recording tools**
Dinosaurs	Plastic food bags	Talking tins
Play people, etc.	Boxes	Talking clipboards
	Spoons	Journey Stick (metre stick on which to stick objects in the order they were found to enable children to recall what they did and what they found)
	Scoops	

The place of loose parts in children's mathematical development

The term 'loose parts' was originally used by a British architect, Simon Nicholson, to talk about materials that could be used in a very open-ended way. Daly and Beloglovsky (2016) show how, through their investigations and explorations of materials, infants and toddlers are gaining in cognitive development in a similar way to heuristic play. Experiences with loose parts allow children to be in control, deepen their critical thinking skills and generate new and creative ideas in solving problems. In this book, there are very clear links made to early stages of mathematical development as children make exciting discoveries about what these objects can do and what they can do with them. Amongst the key skills that can be developed are:

- causality – determining cause and effect, and finding out 'what happens if...' through their play
- classification – recognising which things are the same and not the same in different ways
- seriation – finding that objects can be arranged or lined up in a logical order according to differences, e.g. shortest to tallest
- number concepts – filling, pouring and finding out about quantities
- spatial relations – learning how objects relate to each other and creating connections.

There are also some very strong links made to schematic patterns of behaviour, as discussed in Chapter 1.

Developing the mathematical potential using number tracks outside

At the heart of developing confidence in early counting is the need for children to be engaged in experiences which promote the visualisation of concepts in a way that physically involves them in playing on and investigating number tracks on the ground. Tracks will normally start with simple objects which enable children to move from one space to another, e.g. logs, stepping stones, tyres, and crates or large blocks joined together, and walking over and into these. There may be no numbers involved but even at this stage, the tracks support understanding of:

Spatial awareness: where children start and finish, where they are in relation to each other, working out how near they are to the end, adding on more block or floor tile to extend the track further. The link between this early experience and, later, the matching of numbers and recognition of numerals is the beginning of place value through play-based learning. The language that they use may be more general in discussing who is far away, who is next to, whom they can catch up with, etc. This forms the foundations of a child's ability to visualise where numbers are in relation to each other. If we provide a starting line or circle, they also begin to see a link between a place before one and zero.

Counting on and counting back: being able to relate counting on and back with a one-to-one correspondence using or through the rules of a game in play. These rules often include allowing only one person on a log or in a tyre at the one time, usually due to safety and the size of space.

Making links with a place and a number count: as they begin to apply the skills of reciting numbers practised in rhymes, songs and other play activities, children can now see the purpose of giving each step of the track a number count, and they may ask for numbers to go alongside the track or want to mark make on the track. At this stage some children may relate 0 to the start of a track, often depending on their familiarity with rhymes and songs that count down or back from 5. The language of 'none', 'all gone', 'nothing', even 'blast off', begins to support this concept visually.

Recognition of the numerals in context and visualising which numbers are before, after, in the middle, towards the end, at the beginning: when children are using a number track in a more focused way, they begin to link the number name with its place in ordering the number after, before, then in between. In other contexts of lining up they may have been practising this concept and beginning to link it to first, second, third, last in ordering themselves, following a routine, perhaps at the snack area or in play contexts where this takes on new meaning. They also may begin an early concept of rounding if they talk about the numbers that are near to the end as 10 or near to the beginning as 3.

Links to **one more and one less** as the number after or before: at this stage, children begin to show greater understanding of the link between the number after as one more step, the link with moving on one more as adding and may begin to generate the pattern of adding on 1 and jumping to the next number. The concept of one less as the number before and moving back one is slightly more sophisticated as generally early subtraction begins with the concept of 'take away'. With sufficient meaningful experiences and appropriate and sensitive adult interactions, this link becomes more evident to children.

Problem solving by working out the **difference in the number** of steps from one place to another: for example, how many steps are there to get from 2 to 6? As a problem solving challenge which arises from play, children will see the significance in counting on one step at a time to be 'in the same place' as their friend. This not only links to addition $(2 + 4 = 6)$ but to the very abstract problem with which children find difficulty at a later stage when they are asked to solve $2 + \square = 6$. The value of play and early counting on the number track is strengthened by quality experiences in different contexts indoors and with more space and different opportunities outdoors. Children who are motivated in counting will then want to count on to larger quantities and further explore number patterns in order at their own pace.

Photo 5.9 I wonder how many there are.

Developing the mathematical potential of a washing line outside

Where number tracks are normally created with children moving up and down in a vertical line, the washing line lends itself to a horizontal layout. This may be used initially in the real context of hanging up washing, using the language of 'first, next, then, after', and, if there is nothing left in the bag or basket, using the language of 'none left'. A very subtle way of linking this informally with the concept of the place of zero and the quantity of nothing is to hang up the empty basket at the extreme left-hand side of the line.

Threading balls onto a long line and attaching it onto an outdoor surface can extend this. In this way, children can move the balls along the line by walking with them or

by touching, counting and physically moving each one as they count.
children to use the language of 'lots, more there, some here,' etc. This
outdoor abacus which helps children to start talking about quantities a.
quantitative language.

To extend this experience, children may wish to select the order and colours of the
balls to create a sequence, thread the balls in twos, and possibly move them to create a
repeated pattern, e.g. two red, two blue. For many children, the motivating factor to do
this is from watching others in their play in an open space with such a resource as a focal
point in the outdoor environment. When the motivation is intrinsic and the experience
presented to them is balanced in a more developmentally appropriate way, then many
children may see this highly mathematical experience as yet another place to play. The
key to progression lies in our ability, first of all, to observe children in their play, and
also to know mathematically which are the next steps or possible lines of development.
Using wellies as a context for counting also provides an extension for matching and for
counting in pairs or twos, and looking out for odd wellies!

The washing line may also be used to peg up pictures in order of quantity, and this
may be linked to the current interests of the children or using pictures of the resources
outdoors. Again, the progression in using pictures to develop an understanding of quantity would be as follows:

1   Pictures of the same objects but different quantities in order on the line, e.g. no
    balls, 1 ball, 2 balls, 3 balls. This also means that the cards may be used flexibly for
    a number (quantity) hunt or to find the quantity that is missing.

2   Pictures of the same objects but changed for each quantity, e.g. 1 ball, 2 crates,
    3 tyres, 4 twigs – again, keeping a card with nothing on it to be used at the start
    of the sequence. It would be helpful to involve the children in the selection of the
    photos to be used to increase the ownership of this experience and a talking point
    about who took each photo.

3   Pictures with different objects on each card, e.g. 1 ball, a picture or photo with
    a crate and a tyre as 2 'things', and 3 being depicted by a ball, a tyre and a
    twig. This stage reinforces the abstraction principle, outlined in Chapter 3, when
    children realise anything can be counted, and it also leads into the next stage of
    numerals only.

4   Numeral cards at this stage begin to take on more meaning if children have made
    the links between a quantity, its place on the line and that anything with that quan-
    tity is represented by the numeral as a symbol. Without exploring the depth in this
    experience, we may assume that children have a real understating of the links and
    connections that lie behind these pictures, and that when they see 0, 1, 2, 3, 4, 5,
    they can make automatic links with the associated quantities and relationships
    between them.

Table 5.11 Context for learning

Context for learning	Key skills in mathematical thinking	Possible prompts for thinking

Children's learning

Children's comments

Evaluation and next steps

Points for reflection and discussion

1   Consider the most effective ways to plan for the storage of resources to enable children to see what is on offer. Think about the range of resources. Are there too many or too few? How can you be responsive to the children's own ideas?

2   Look back over some of the contexts in Tables 5.1–5.10. Can you think of other possible lines of development in resourcing for early mathematical development?

3   Select a story that has mathematical possibilities within it. How could this content provide play opportunities for children to make links and connections?

4   If you were to follow a child's lead in wanting a sensory garden, garden centre or fairy garden, how could you take this forward?

References

Daly, L. and Beloglovsky, M. (2016) *Loose Parts 2: Inspiring Play with Infants and Toddlers*. St Paul, MN. Redleaf Press.

Ginsberg, G. (2006) 'Mathematical Play and Playful Mathematics: A Guide for Early Education.' In Singer, D., Golinkoff, M.G. and Hirsh-Pasek, K. (eds.), *Play = Learning. How Play Motivates and Enhances Children's Cognitive and Social- Emotional Growth*. New York. Oxford University Press, pp. 145–165.

Keith, L. and Mosley, F. (2012) *Planning and Progression Guide Early Level*. Heinemann Active Maths. Pearson Education Ltd.

Keith, L. and Mosley, F. (2016) *Teaching Guide Foundation*. Heinemann Active Maths Northern Ireland. Pearson Education Ltd.

Leicestershire County Council (2017) 'Outdoor Learning.' Available at https://resources.leicester shire.gov.uk/education-and-children/early-learning-and-childcare/childcare-practice/teaching-learning-and-assessment/outdoor-learning

Stevens, J. (2008) *Maths in Stories*. London. BEAM Education.

Further reading and websites

CCEA, Learning Outdoors in the Early Years

DCSF (2009) Children Thinking Mathematically PSRN Essential Knowledge for Early Years Practitioners. London.

Early Years Outdoor Learning: A Toolkit for Developing Early Years Outdoor Provision (2009) www.norfolk.gov.uk/outdoorlearning

First Steps Outdoors (Welsh Government and Learning through Landscapes, 2010)

Grounds for Learning www.ltl.org.uk/scotland and www.gflscotland.org.uk

Learning through Landscapes www.ltl.org.uk

Nicholson, S. (1971) The Theory of Loose Parts on www.letthechildrenplay.net

Outdoors Matters! www.outdoormatters.co.uk

Play Wales www.playwales.org.uk

Play Scotland www.playscotland.org.uk

Play England www.playengland.org.uk

Shared Vision and Value for Outdoor Play in the Early Years www.tinyurl.com/visionvalues

Skinner, C. (2005) *Maths Outdoors*. London. BEAM Education.

6 How can we plan for effective learning and quality experiences?

Mrs Keith, my child can count to 10. Can you move him onto 20 now?

—Request from a parent

This chapter builds upon contexts and resources in the previous chapters to focus on key questions in planning and starting from the child's interests. It will explore the wider issues in taking the pedagogy into practice and end with a case study to illustrate children's involvement in the planning process of creating a junkyard garden. Key questions will include:

- What makes a quality experience in early mathematical development?
- How can we develop a culture of challenge with young children?
- What does differentiation look like in practice?
- How will we plan but be responsive to the child's involvement in the process? What are some possible starting points?
- How can the plan be recorded with the appropriate links to the curriculum?
- How will we observe and record the child's learning journey?
- How will we plan for next steps?

What makes a quality experience in early mathematical development?

A quality experience in early mathematical development:

- involves adult interactions and young children's sustained shared thinking through their real engagement in the process
- motivates children in the process and joy of playful learning

- develops the underpinning skills in early mathematical development in a natural way and from the child's curiosity; our role is to make quality observations based on knowledge of those skills, the curriculum within which we work and the stages of development in each aspect of maths

- promotes positive attitudes to learning mathematically and offers some element of self-challenge to children.

- Allows the children to take risks within a safe and secure mathematical learning environment

- provides scope to connect different areas of early mathematical awareness and also across areas of learning

- is supported by open-ended resources which are flexible in how they may be used and adapted, enabling children to combine resources for their own purposes and develop their own ideas and plans

- provides a memorable experience that children can recall at a later date

- promotes problem solving skills and capabilities, allowing time for them to work something out and to think through a process.

Developing a culture of challenge

If young children have a natural curiosity and want to find something out, we have to look at the links of how they not only face challenges in their play, but how they develop positive attitudes and see challenge as exciting. When working with primary pupils on a challenging task and asking them what the word 'challenge' means, I often hear responses that it is hard, stressful, and they have to think too much, so we need to consider that by using the language of challenge in our everyday language, a change in mindset in the early years could support children in their resilience and persistence in meeting challenge. Challenges may be part of the outdoor area in what and how experiences are offered, in an implicit and embedded way. There may be times when a more explicit challenge may meet the needs of children who want to attempt these. There are many children who thrive on challenge, and no more so than when involved in competitive games. After talk on this subject on one of my courses, some staff set up a 'challenge table', starting very simply with a challenge of the week, for example, *Can you move the pebbles from the tray into the bucket with large tweezers?* After some discussion about what they may have to think about in this challenge, staff were surprised at how many children wanted to join in and then started to come up with ideas for their challenges. In one setting, this led to a 'challenge of the week' book where children could take their own photos and record what they did to achieve the challenge. More surprisingly, parents and carers became interested in what was going on as children were wearing 'I met the challenge' stickers and this, in itself, led to informal discussions about what and how the children were learning in a mathematical way. The whole experience led to a challenge wall and challenges happening indoors and outside. There may also be scope in offering even young children different levels of challenge. In primary school maths, where I have been investigating children making choices in challenges, I am amazed at how many actually want to strive for the difficult challenges. Depending on the challenge, this is an excellent opportunity to discuss the skills needed to attempt the challenge, confidence levels to try something but not worry if it doesn't work out the first time and the acceptance that it may be easier to go back to a simpler challenge and work up again to the more difficult one. If this is the type of mathematical thinker that we want in the later stages of the primary school, then the attitudes and dispositions to learning mathematically in this way need to be encouraged.

What could this culture of challenge look like in practice and how does it link with the social environment discussed in Chapter 2?

Some indicators may include:

- more open-ended experiences
- children and adults posing open-ended questions
- encouraging a sense of wonder and inquiry
- children posing their own problems
- modelling the thinking process
- children applying skills
- developing positive mindsets to challenge
- children's ability to talk about and reflect upon their learning through the challenge
- children's ability to record their thinking in different ways and sometimes in markmaking during the process
- developing depth in thinking with children talk about the process as well as the
- outcome of the challenge.

What is differentiation in early mathematical development, and how can we use this to meet the needs of all children on their learning journeys?

Differentiation is often thought of as giving children a more difficult task or just moving them onto more difficult concepts, but it involves more than this. Our observations are central to knowing where children are at mathematically, how they engage in the mathematical learning, their interest and curiosity to find out more. We can differentiate in many different ways:

- by accepting that children will have different learning styles: they will need different resources to support them in their learning, different levels of motivation and confidence and very different levels in making connections

- by providing and suggesting resources that may interest the child and asking for their own suggestions about props in their play
- by questioning and interacting in different ways depending on the level of general and specific mathematical language development of each child
- by the pace at which we introduce new learning and the acceptance that children need the time to revisit mathematical concepts in different ways and with different regularity
- by the feedback that we customise to each child's level so that the focus in feedback is directly on what and how they have been learning

This leads to the question of what we are actually assessing in children's mathematical learning outdoors. In making a quality observation of what is significant in how they are learning, it may be useful to consider the following concepts:

- dispositions to learning: what attitudes are children demonstrating through their play?
- progression in development of concepts and understanding: What concepts are children developing through the experiences? What do you notice that is new or different to show their understanding?
- ability to make links in their learning and build on previous experiences
- ability to discuss learning and communicating their ideas in different ways
- skill development: what skills are the children using and applying in different play contexts?

Therefore, in our observations outdoors, we can begin to think about how a child starts or enters an experience. In monitoring where they go and with whom and what they interact (including adults), we can continue to develop our own knowledge of a young child as a mathematical thinker.

Taking outdoor planning forward

Starting from a question and asking more questions

Context for planning

Let's have a teddy bears' picnic. What do we need to think about?

If our aim is to engage children in the planning process, we can start with a question and see where the mathematical learning takes us. Starting with a blank sheet of paper or in a large planning book, take the children's suggestions for questions and record these in one colour on some sticky notes. At a later stage, sort the questions on the notes into the different aspects or headings for maths that you use to see the overall balance of the context. If there is a particular focus that you think would be useful, then add this as an adult-initiated question, but don't detract from the children's ideas or create links which are not meaningful.

Observations can then be added to a very basic overall plan, but new ideas generated from the children or problems encountered in the planning and implementation of the teddies' picnic can be added in a final colour to show the learning journey. If this has been a successful context outdoors, then leave the resources you've made for free play when children want to take the teddies somewhere else.

Some possible questions that may arise or can be explored:

- Number and counting
  - How many teddies will there be?
  - Which teddies will we invite? Why?
  - What rhymes do the teddies like to sing?
  - What do we need (plates, cups)? How many of each?
  - Do the teddies need to line up to go to the picnic? What will be the order? Who will be first?

- Shape, position and movement
  - How will the bears get to the picnic?
  - How will we set out the picnic?
  - How can we pack the food?
  - What would be a good shape for the basket? Why?
  - Can we make a treasure hunt for the teddies? Where will we hide the treasure?

- Time
  - Let's make a timetable of what they will do.
  - What time will the picnic start and how long will it last?

- Measure
  - Do we have a blanket big enough for all the teddies to sit on?
  - Do we need to weigh anything?
  - What if the basket is too heavy?

- Money
  - Do we need to buy anything?
  - How will we pay for it?
  - How much will it cost?

- Information handling
  - What will the teddies want to eat?
  - How can we find out which games to play? Does everyone have a favourite game?
  - How could we record this?

- Reflecting
  - Which part of the picnic did you enjoy best? Why?
  - If we had another picnic, would you suggest anything else?
  - What else could we plan for the teddies?

Starting from a resource and possible question for investigation

Context for planning: we have some new cable drums and nuts and bolts. What can we do with them?

Planning may also arise from the excitement of a new resource or with a resource that can be combined to change children's mathematical play. As this is a good opportunity to observe children at the exploration stage with the resource, you may find the process and skills overview (Table 6.1) a useful planning tool for observation comments and using these to inform next steps in your planning.

Photo 6.1 What can we find out?

Table 6.1 Taking maths outdoors: mathematical processes and skills

Deciding	Reasoning	Predicting
Imagining	Planning	Cause and effect
Exploring strategies	Talking about and sharing ideas	Evaluating
Problem solving	Explaining	Comparing
Measuring	Refining ideas	Visualising
Sorting	Making choices and decisions	Applying skills in different contexts
Estimating	Sharing	Counting
Justifying	Sequencing and ordering	Recording
Observations and possible lines of development		

Table 6.2 Creating a rich environment for early mathematical awareness outdoors

Bikes and tracks	Mud kitchen	Plants and growing	Sand/water investigations
Den building	Large construction	Loose parts centre	Physical play
Observations			

Photo 6.2 There was once a nursery garden

St Luke's primary early years, class, November–March

The project began with a letter sent to parents and carers to inform them that the staff team and children were in the process of developing a garden area into a junkyard garden. Children had been consulted, and together they had negotiated rules to keep safe. Their intention was to further develop a 'loose part' approach with the underpinning belief that such an environment would empower the children's creativity. They set out to source loose parts, e.g. milk crates, pallets, guttering, bread crates, carpet samples, cable reels, old utensils, logs, left over decking, metal buckets, bore pipes and old/ unused metal teapots.

The children then came up with the following ideas:

- An explorer camp, you can't see us but we can see the animals.
- I could make a shelter and a hide-out.
- A jungle. A dinosaur land.
- A fairyland in the trees and bushes.
- A dragon land, a land for wizards too.
- On the circle you pile up stuff and make a castle.
- You can sit down on the blocks for a wee rest.

- You can run along the fence with a stick and make music. Remember we did that.
- It would be good for a den.
- We could grow things.
- You can make a bug house, and then all the bugs would come.
- Just play with your friends.

They went out to visit other junkyard gardens to get more ideas. They liked the music walls (see Photos 6.3 and 6.4).

The children's ideas were then extended with many more suggestions as they recalled and recorded their visits.

In January, the nursery had acquired a new fence and gates so the garden was safe and secure. Children and staff looked again at the outdoor/garden rules to see whether any further changes or additions were necessary. There was also a set of rules for teachers and other adults!

- You always have to count and look after each other.
- Any broken bits, the teachers have to take them away.
- The teachers listen. They like to hear laughing. They don't like to hear us crying.

Photo 6.3 The music wall

Photo 6.4 We like this wall, too

- They can use the walkie-talkies.
- Someone writes how many children are going out. That's to keep us safe.

The tyres arrived and children had to work out how to get these into the junkyard garden. With the help of the St Luke's Primary Learning Council, a special project began to build a bug hotel out of recycled materials. They started with a large pallet and then gathered sticks for the 'ants to crawl along', and with help, they cut plastic bottles 'for the bugs to sleep in and eat leaves'.

Another problem arose when some logs arrived from the tree surgeons who were cutting down some trees after a storm. The question posed was, *How are we going to get them to the junkyard garden?* Comments included:

- Teamwork, we can go in teams.
- Get a lorry!
- We could use the wheelbarrows.
- Let's all have a think about it.

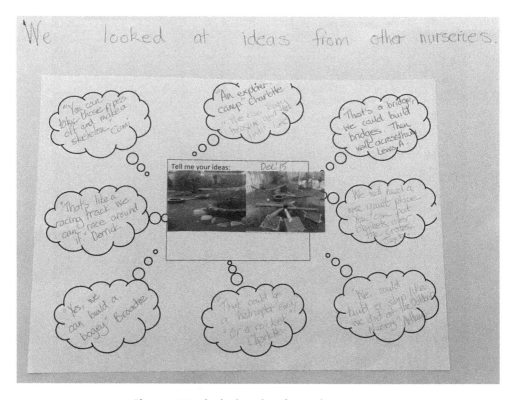

Photo 6.5 We looked at ideas from other nurseries

After trying unsuccessfully to lift them, then roll them, they discovered a trolley that could help solve the problem.

They then decided to create a Maths and Numeracy Wall with drop tubes and differently numbered balls to go through, willow for dens and measuring, and balanced scales attached to the fencing. This led to many different lines of possible development, especially in the challenge to feed through some plastic balls to make a long line. The children showed particular concentration and perseverance in their contributions to this task:

- The holes were tiny, and you had to concentrate.
- I was getting in a tangle.

In making the Water Wall, children were involved in attaching funnels to piping and testing it out. When the cable reels arrived the children were asked how they could be used.

- It could be a racing car steering wheel.
- A wee table for the fairies.

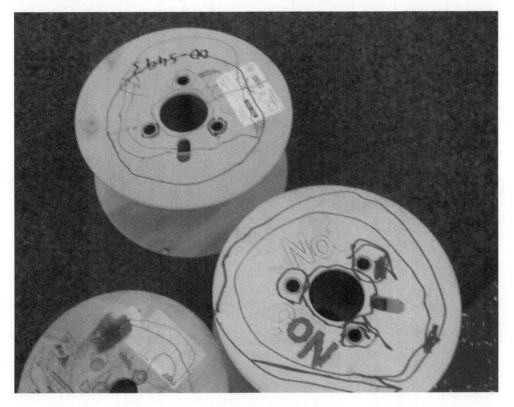

Photo 6.6 How could we use these?

- Wheels for a bus.
- Drums, you can play the drums.
- A seat to sit on while you are getting your wellies on.
- I saw 4 circles on mine. You could put a rope through.
- Roll it down the path.

The children invited all their parents and carers to the official opening of the junkyard garden to celebrate their successes and to show how proud they were of their achievements. Parents and carers were encouraged to dress appropriately for a 'stay and play' session and join in the fun!

Not surprisingly the children continued to come up with new ideas and developments, and they recorded all of this. In the final pages of the large floor book to record our story, there is an excellent link to the well-being indicators underpinning the curriculum in Scotland, and staff have also evaluated the environment in line with *Building the Ambition: National Practice Guidance on Early Learning and Children and Young People* (Scottish Government, 2014).

Table 6.3 St Luke's Primary children's views

St Luke's Early Years Class Kilwinning
These are collated responses and expressions of views from the children as we discussed the well-being indicators in small informal groups throughout the junkyard garden project. Each child made a contribution to these agreed statements. There are many more in our outdoor learning floor book. March 2016

S Safe	H Healthy	A Achieving	N Nurtured	A Active	R Respected	R Responsible	I Included
We have fences and gates to keep us safe.	Being outside in the fresh air is good for you.	There was nothing in the garden, now we have a junkyard garden and lots of things to do!	The ladies look after us and we look after our friends.	We are always very busy in the junkyard garden!	The grown-ups and my friends listen to my ideas and I listen to theirs.	We tidy up the garden too, just like in nursery.	Everyone helped make all the things for the garden and we all helped put it altogether.
We check all the things before we go out and the teachers have special checks to do too.	We always have a healthy snack. We have to do a lot of thinking and that keeps your brain healthy.	We helped make some of the things in the garden. I have big muscles now because it was hard work making and building all the things.	If we have a good idea, we can ask the ladies to help us, sometimes we just ask our friends.	You use your body and your brain to think up good ideas and solve problems. I like being outside for a long time.	I sometimes have to wait for a turn of my favourite bit.	If we see anything broken, we have to tell a grown-up. We take turns and share.	Everybody gets a chance to play in the junkyard garden, even the Mums and Dads!
We look after each other. We are safe using tools.		It is so good, the big boys and girls want to play!	If we have a good idea the teachers say 'That's a great idea, let's do it!'		We talk a lot about what we want to do but if you don't want to go out you don't need to.	We keep our looking eyes and listening ears switched on.	If someone has no one to play with, we can say, 'Come and play with us.'

St Luke's Early Years Class Kilwinning
Getting It Right for Every Child (Staff Records)

Table 6.4 St Luke's Primary staff views

S Safe	H Healthy	A Achieving	N Nurtured	A Active	R Respected	R Responsible	I Included
The children and staff have clear, negotiated rules and routines for safety.	Playing outside offers may health benefits: Physical health Active play Physical fitness Physical development Large muscle development Sunlight Fresh air Healthy snacks Mental and emotional health Ideas listened to and respected Praise given. Children are aware of good hygiene and general safety outdoors.	Becoming more independent in dressing. Learning new skills and persevering with tasks. Building up stamina and resilience. Working as part of a team to accomplish a task. Being more aware of your achievements and sharing them with your family.	Involve children in the process of how we make this environment safe, fun and inspiring. Knowing that the adults will listen to their ideas and help them take these forward. Creating a sense of ownership of the junkyard garden by involving the children every step of the way. Praise the children for playing well together, sharing, turn taking, etc.	Daily opportunities for children to be active outdoors. Learning and practising new skills. Being outdoors in all weathers and being aware of how this can make them feel. Exploring the different areas available for outdoor learning. Many opportunities to be mentally active, thinking, reasoning, planning and testing.	Adults really listen to children's ideas and through discussion, support, taking these ideas forward if at all possible. Encourage children to respect each other's views. Turn taking and sharing. Ensure that there is choice for children. Share the children's achievements with other children, staff in class and school, families and local community. Mark the children's achievements with a celebration for children and their families. Encourage children to respect the environment they have created and the school environment.	Children are given opportunities to learn new skills, have responsibility for certain tasks, be part of a big project and so have ownership of the junkyard garden. Children made and set up the environment, made decisions about where things would work best and agreed arrangements for tidy up-time. The children were consulted on rules for outdoor learning and negotiated rules for themselves and staff. Children are encouraged to be a good teammate and support their friends. The children have spent a lots of time practising getting dressed/undressed for outdoors. They can also change to dry socks, etc. if required.	All the children have been consulted on the junkyard garden project. We have encouraged the children to value each other's contributions. Each child has contributed both verbally with their ideas and physically with the design and creation of the areas. Every child has had opportunities to be part of the project and eventually spent whole sessions in the junkyard garden.
Looking after ourselves, each other and contents of the junkyard garden are discussed on a regular basis (informal risk assessments daily). Formal risk benefits and risk assessments completed.							

Table 6.5 Junkyard garden

Building the ambition: How can we use its advice to review our environments for early learning?

Well-being	Communication	Curiosity, inquiry and creativity
Gives a balance of being in and out of doors so that children are confident in different environments.	Provides areas for children to engage in conversations, small cosy spaces, occasional large groups to talk, listen and share their ideas.	Encourages inquiry and invites discussion and exploration with interesting objects to talk about and explore, stimulating curiosity.
Organises resources which enable children to make choices, and share in others' choices.	Is rich in opportunities for children to engage in conversations, imagine and create, find out and reason answers.	Is supportive of giving time for the young child to persevere with their thinking and inquiries, to test their own theories out over several days or re-examine the same experience again over time in a variety of ways.
Resources which are clearly labelled and where children know to find and replace them.		
Has comfortable places to relax, be quiet and be with friends.	Encourages conversation about the here and now, the past and future and discussions about the world around them.	
Has plenty for the young child to talk about, imagining and creating, reasoning and testing out, sharing and negotiating, talking about the past, present and the future.	Has a library rich in books, favourite stories, fiction and non-fiction books, books children have made themselves, recordings of experiences and stories they want to share and tell.	Offers daily access outside to the wider environment which is rich in opportunities for inquiry learning.
Reflects the world of print, literacy and numeracy and the increasing use of technologies to support learning.	Uses environmental print recognisable to children to help a growing understanding that print has meaning.	Is well organised to allow young children the freedom to select equipment and materials that they want and also appreciate the need to accommodate the choices of others.
Gives time to persevere with inquiry learning and time to start a project and continue it over several days.	Uses technologies to widen children's experiences of different methods.	

Building the ambition: How can we use its advice to review our environments for early learning?

Well-being	Communication	Curiosity, inquiry and creativity
Experiences which:		**Adults who:**
• Encourage children to try out new things, using children's interest as a starting point.		• Encourage a young child's learning by suggesting they try things out, inspire curiosity and see that it is essential to how children learn.
• Are new and stimulate enthusiasm, new learning and curiosity, balanced with more familiar experiences which can be revisited and tested out in different ways. Develop a sense of risk.		• Help children make sensible choices about their learning by involving them in making decisions about what could be provided and evaluating their own experiences.
• Allow children to determine what they want to learn, form their own plans and gives ownership in discussion with an adult when they want to stop.		
• Provide opportunities that encourage children's understanding of living things and the local and natural environment.		• Make time to talk and listen to what a young child is saying and try to build on their meaning and reply in a way that children will understand but also models new language and descriptions.
• Help the young child to remember how they have used materials and solved problems in the past and how they can relate this learning to the task in hand.		
• Give children a sense of wonder and stimulate questioning and ability to reason and test conclusions.		• Are not afraid to change their own plans and take the lead from the child and who are able to act as a support to the young child when needed.
• Allow children to play outside, fresh air and exercise.		• Understand children will start at different points and encourage them to try activities at the appropriate level.

Source: Adapted from *Building the Ambition: National Practice Guidance on Early Learning and Childcare Guidelines*, Scottish Government (2014).

Table 6.6 Taking maths outdoors

Anticipated experience	
Key skills and possible focus for learning	**Questions to promote children's thinking**
What we observed	
Possible lines of development	

Table 6.7 Linking the outcomes and experiences, key skills and processes and key prompts in a holistic way

I am developing a sense of size and amount by observing, exploring, using and communicating with others about things in the world around me. **MNU 0–01a** — *Have we enough? Who has more? How many do you think we need?*	I am developing my awareness of how money is used and can recognise and use a range of coins. **MNU 0–09a** — *What do we need to set up a…shop? Where do we need money outside?*	I am aware of how routines and events in my world link with times and seasons, and have explored ways to record and display these using clocks, calendars and other methods. **MNU 0–10a** — *How can we make an autumn picture?*	I have experimented with everyday items as units of measure to investigate and compare sizes and amounts in my environment, sharing my findings with others. **MNU 0–11a** — *This is too heavy. How can I make it lighter?*	I have spotted and explored patterns in my own and the wider environment and can copy and continue these and create my own patterns. **MTH 0–13a** — *What types of pattern can I see outside?*

Taking maths outdoors
Mathematical processes and skills

Deciding	Imagining	Predicting	
Reasoning	Planning		Cause and effect
Exploring strategies	Talking about and sharing ideas		Evaluating
Explaining	Comparing		Problem solving
Trying out different strategies	Sorting		Measuring
Making choices and decisions	Applying skills in different contexts		Visualising
Estimating	Refining ideas		Justifying
Sharing	Counting		Recording
Sequencing and ordering	Locating		

I have explored numbers, understanding that they represent quantities, and I can use them to count, create sequences and describe order. **MNU 0–02a** — *How can I find out how many there are? What will happen if I put on 1 more?*	I use practical materials and can 'count on and back' to help me to understand addition and subtraction, recording my ideas and solutions in different ways. **MNU 0–03a** — *How can I make a game to count on and back?*	I can share out a group of items by making smaller groups and can split a whole object into smaller parts. **MNU 0–07a** — *How can we make it fair? Is there the same quantity in each?*	I enjoy investigating objects and shapes and can sort, describe and be creative with them. **MTH 0–16a** — *What objects can I use to build? What will I need?* In movement, games, and using technology I can use simple directions and describe positions. **MTH 0–17a** — *How can I get to…? How can I give directions to?* I have had fun creating a range of symmetrical pictures and patterns using a range of media. **MTH 0–19a** — *What can I use to make a symmetrical picture?*	

(Continued)

Table 6.7 (Continued)

I can collect objects and ask questions to gather information, organising and displaying my findings in different ways. **MNU 0–20a** *How can I record my sorting?* *What questions do I need to ask?*	I can match objects, and sort using my own and others' criteria, sharing my ideas with others. **MNU 0–20b** *What can I sort?* *How can I sort it?*	I can use the signs and charts around me for information, helping me plan and make choices and decisions in my daily life. **MNU 0–20c** *What signs do we need?* *How can I make one?*

Points for reflection and discussion

1   How will you take forward your own thinking about what makes a quality experience?

2   How can you take the planning forward in outdoor learning in early maths?

3   What main issues arise from this chapter for your own learning and professional development?

Reference

Scottish Government (2014) *Building the Ambition: National Practice Guidance on Early Learning and Childcare, Children and Young People (Scotland) Act 2014.* Edinburgh. APS Group Scotland.

Drawing conclusions and taking it forward: implications for your own professional development

In this final chapter, key issues from the book will be addressed through a self-evaluation toolkit to audit implications for professional development and in taking forward the ideas from this book. It will enable you to bring together your final thoughts in linking pedagogy of early mathematical awareness and play and enable you to reflect on the next steps for your own professional development.

Table 7.1 Reflections on Chapter 1

Overview and key questions

What types of young mathematical learners do we want?

How do our young children learn best mathematically?

Why take maths outdoors?

Key points for reflection at the end of the chapter

- What are your own experiences of and feelings about maths?
- How might these influence your work with young children?
- What recurring themes of how young children learn best in maths arise in this chapter?
- How can we start to think about how to support young children as mathematical learners?

Overall points for reflection and next steps for your own practice

Table 7.2 Reflections on Chapter 2

Overview and key questions

What do we need to consider in developing a mathematically rich outdoor learning environment?

What should the physical layout of the space that we have available in the immediate outdoors and beyond look like?

What experiences should occur there to support children in what they are learning and how they are developing their mathematical learning?

Key points for reflection at the end of the chapter

1   How do we provide opportunities for the children to explore mathematically outdoors in such a way that they are motivated to want to learn, revisit, apply and become creative in their thinking and in developing their own ideas?

2   Do we create an atmosphere where exploration and 'having a go' are seen as just as important as getting a correct answer?

3   Do we provide a rich and interesting environment and plenty of experiences where there will be lots of opportunities for problem solving to be embedded as an approach in developing early mathematical awareness and in children developing confidence?

4   Look again at the 12 features of a quality mathematical environment outdoors, and discuss other ways to take each feature forward.

5   Using the tables in this chapter, try to think of some more resources or mathematical ideas that may arise from the children's play.

Overall points for reflection and next steps for your own practice

---

Table 7.3 Reflections on Chapter 3

Overview and key questions

What are the key stages in mathematical development?

What is the place of problem solving through play?

Key points for reflection at the end of the chapter

1   What do you notice about the different ways in which early maths is represented in each curriculum design?

2   What ideas can you take from this chapter to motivate children in their mathematical learning?

3   How would you set up a new problem for children to investigate or respond to children who want to find out something?

Overall points for refection and next steps for your own practice

Table 7.4 Reflections on Chapter 4

Overview and key questions

How can we support young children in their learning?

What makes effective questioning? How can we help to support children in planning, reviewing and evaluating their learning through mathematical conversations?

How valuable is children's own mark making in helping them make sense of the mathematical world?

Key points for reflection at the end of the chapter

1   How can we develop more shared sustained thinking with children to develop maths conversations?

2   How can we develop our own questioning techniques and have a shared understanding of key prompts for thinking?

3   How can we further the importance of mark making in children's mathematical play?

Overall points for refection and next steps for your own practice

Table 7.5 Reflections on Chapter 5

Overview and key questions

What resources can support and enhance mathematical learning outdoors?

What makes an effective context for learning in early mathematical awareness outdoors?

What is the mathematical potential of the resources we have and how they are used?

What is the value of number tracks and washing lines?

Key points for reflection at the end of the chapter

1   Consider the most effective ways to plan for the storage of resources to enable children to see what is on offer. Think about the range of resources. Are there too many or too few? How can you be responsive to the children's own ideas?

2   Look back over some of the contexts in Tables 5.1–5.10. Can you think of other possible lines of development in resourcing for early mathematical development?

3   Select a story that has mathematical possibilities within it. How could this content provide play opportunities for children to make links and connections?

4   If you were to follow a child's lead in wanting a sensory garden, garden centre or fairy garden, how could you take this forward?

Overall points for refection and next steps for your own practice

Table 7.6 Reflections on Chapter 6

Overview and key questions

What makes a quality experience in early mathematical development?

How can we develop a culture of challenge with young children?

What does differentiation look like in practice?

How will we plan but be responsive to the child's involvement in the process?

What are some possible starting points?

How can the plan be recorded with the appropriate links to the curriculum?

How will we observe and record the child's learning journey?

How will we plan for next steps?

Key points for reflection at the end of the chapter

1   How will you take forward your own thinking about what makes a quality experience?

2   How can you take the planning forward in outdoor learning in early maths?

3   What main issues arise from this chapter for your own learning and professional development?

Overall points for refection and next steps for your own practice

---

So why take maths outdoors as a context for early mathematical development? Curriculum for Excellence (Scotland) is underpinned by four capacities develop all learners to become: successful learners, confident individuals, responsible citizens and effective contributors. No matter where we work with young children or to which curriculum or guidelines, it is hoped that these underpinning values would be embedded in our practice.

If we were to apply the key messages from this book, consider how we could define what these four capacities may look like in practice:

Successful learners

- Different environment for learning
- A place to apply, extend and develop new learning
- Develop conceptual understanding in the real world
- Increase motivation and relevance of maths at these vital stages
- Children talking about what they have discovered outdoors
- Thinking creatively and seeing new ways to learn in different environments

Confident individuals

- Developing thinking skills
- Asking new and different questions
- Reflecting on their learning
- Making choices and mathematical decisions
- Motivated to learn mathematically

Responsible citizens

- Working collaboratively
- Negotiating on a larger scale
- Sharing their findings and learning from each other
- Recognising and becoming more aware of maths in everyday life
- Developing a love of the outdoors and a love of learning

Effective contributors

- Using their initiative and taking risks to learn new things
- Developing a 'can do' approach to maths
- Developing independence in thought through the early years
- Having a sense of purpose and ownership through their mathematical play

Index

Note: Page number in **bold** type refer to **figures**
Page numbers in *italic* type refer to *tables*
Page numbers followed by 'P' refer to photos